**W9-BFD-373**

# 200
## STUDENT MEALS

HAMLYN **ALL COLOR COOKBOOK**

# 200 STUDENT MEALS

**SARA LEWIS**

An Hachette UK Company
www.hachette.co.uk

First published in Great Britain in 2011 by Hamlyn,
a division of Octopus Publishing Group Ltd,
Carmelite House, 50 Victoria Embankment,
London EC4Y 0DZ
www.octopusbooks.co.uk
www.octopusbooksusa.com

This edition published in 2016

Copyright © Octopus Publishing Group Ltd 2011, 2016
Distributed in the US by Hachette Book Group,
1290 Avenue of the Americas, 4th and 5th Floors,
New York, NY 10020

Distributed in Canada by Canadian Manda Group,

664 Annette St., Toronto, Ontario, Canada M6S 2C8

ISBN 978-0-600-63359-4

Printed and bound in China

10 9 8 7 6 5 4 3 2 1

Standard level kitchen cup and spoon measurements are
used in all recipes.

Ovens should be preheated to the specific temperature; if
using a convection oven, follow manufacturer's instructions
for adjusting the time and the temperature.

Eggs should be large unless otherwise stated. The U.S.
Food and Drug Administration advises that eggs should not
be consumed raw. This book contains dishes made with
raw or lightly cooked eggs. It is prudent for more vulnerable
people, such as pregnant and nursing mothers, people with
weakened immune systems, the elderly, babies, and young
children, to avoid uncooked or lightly cooked dishes made
with eggs. Once prepared, these dishes should be kept
refrigerated and used promptly.

This book includes dishes made with nuts and nut derivatives.
It is advisable for customers with known allergic reactions to
nuts and nut derivatives and those who may be potentially
vulnerable to these allergies, such as pregnant and nursing
mothers, people with weakened immune systems, the elderly,
babies, and children, to avoid dishes made with nuts and
nut oils. It is also prudent to check the labels of prepared
ingredients for the possible inclusion of nut derivatives.

# contents

# introduction

# introduction

Student food needn't be dull, just because you are on a tight budget. You might have to plan a little more so that the money you do have can go as far as possible but that is perhaps the hardest bit. Anyone can cook and with so many influences from around the world, student food can be as traditional or as exotic as you want it. Gradually build up a pantry of favorite spices and ingredients you use a lot (see opposite for some ideas) and then pick up fresh food as and when you need it.

## essentials to take to college

### cooking equipment

You don't need to spend a fortune to get a basic set of cooking things together. Supermarkets and large department stores have a wide range of basic items and the chances are that your family will have extra pots and pans to donate. Try local thrift stores for bargains, or students who are moving on, who might also want to sell on their items.

## tools and implements

- A cutting board. The cheapest and easiest to store is a plastic board.
- Some basic knives: a large serrated knife for cutting bread and cake, a medium-sized knife for chopping vegetables and cutting meat into pieces, and a small knife for peeling veg and cutting up fruit.
- Everyday cutlery for eating.
- A nonstick skillet—preferably with a lid—is invaluable for fry-ups, stir-fries and omelets.
- A small nonstick saucepan for oatmeal, sauces, or scrambled egg.
- A couple of bowls that stack one inside the other, for mixing salad and beating cakes.
- A couple of heavy-based saucepans with metal handles and lids for on the stove and in the oven.
- A baking sheet, roasting tin, and cake tins.
- A grater with a container below means you can grate more than you need at once.
- A large strainer for draining veg, pasta, rice.
- A veg peeler, a couple of wooden spoons, a turner for turning fried foods, some measuring spoons and cups, a slotted spoon, balloon whisk, a small potato masher, a can opener, and bottle opener.
- Storage containers, a plastic lunch box for eating between studies or lectures, a couple of plastic boxes for the refrigerator that you can label, for storing cheese and dairy things in one, bacon in the other.
- Foil, plastic bags and plastic wrap, to keep those leftovers from drying out.
- Dinner plate, tea plate, and cereal bowl.
- An egg cup.

## basic stores

- Tea, coffee, and hot chocolate
- Onions, potatoes, and garlic
- Sunflower oil
- Salt and pepper
- Vinegar, tomato ketchup
- Bouillon cubes
- Sugar
- All-purpose flour
- Breakfast cereals
- Jelly or spreads
- Cans of tomatoes, baked beans, tuna
- Dried pasta, rice
- Spice—cinnamon, chili, curry powder or separate curry spices (cumin, coriander, turmeric, and garam masala)
- Dried herbs—mixed herbs, oregano, and thyme
- Tomato paste, jar of pesto
- Red or green lentils, couscous, canned or dried legumes
- Emergency jars of pasta sauce, cans of soup
- Milk, butter or spread, yogurts
- Eggs
- Bread
- Bacon or sausages
- Fruit—bananas, apples, or grapes
- Fresh veg—carrots, tomatoes, cucumber, lettuce
- Fresh herbs, bunch of fresh cilantro and potted basil
- Frozen peas or corn
- Frozen mixed summer fruits
- Frozen chicken pieces, ground beef, sausages, fish steaks, shrimp, frozen pizza, garlic bread

**Tip** If fresh herbs go a little limp, soak in cold water for an hour or so then drain and put into a sealed plastic bag and store in a drawer of the refrigerator. They will keep for a week.

## help...funds are low

Here are a few ideas to stretch the remaining ingredients in your store cupboard, as well as use up any fresh foods or leftovers that you have in the fridge when money is short.

### baked potato toppers

Wash and scrub a medium baking potato, then prick with a fork, and wrap with a sheet of paper towel. Place in a microwave for 6 minutes on full power or bake in a pre-heated oven 400°F, for 1 hour or until tender. Sweet potatoes take a little less time. Slit the potato open and top with one of the following:
**Baked beans spiced** up with some chili sauce
**Reheated leftover Bolognese sauce,** sprinkled with grated cheddar cheese.
**A spoonful of cream cheese or yogurt,** drizzled with sweet chili sauce and some torn cilantro leaves.
**Canned tuna** mixed with canned or frozen corn, chopped spring onions and a spoonful of mayonnaise.
**Garlicky tomato sauce** (see page 60)—add some sliced mushrooms and a little fresh basil.

### main meal soups

These are comforting, cheap, and don't require much dishwashing. Fry up a few diced veggies, add stock and canned beans, if you like and simmer until the veg are tender. Serve

as it is or mash if you like your soup smooth. Try flavoring the soup with chili, garlic, fresh herbs, or ground spices—for recipe ideas see Spanish Chickpea Soup on page 32 or White Bean Soup Provencal, page 28.

For another low-cost meal cook up a basic risotto and top with any vegetables you have—roasted butternut squash or cherry tomatoes, steamed broccoli, or garlicky fried sliced mushrooms. Sprinkle with grated Parmesan or crumbled goats' or blue cheese. For those who prefer their rice a little spicier try the Simple Vegetable Biriyani on page 116.

### not just eggs and bacon...

If you have some potatoes, pasta, rice, beans, lentils, or couscous you have the base for as many suppers as you can think of. They're cheap, fill you up, and the carbohydrate in them is complex so they are digested slowly leaving you full for longer. Don't forget to eat fruit and veg – you need vitamin C on a daily basis. If you are low on vitamins you are more likely to go down with colds and miss out on student life! A glass of chilled orange juice is one of your daily fruit portions. Add an apple to your bag and you are on your way. Stir-fries are quick and tasty. You can use whatever you have available – some sliced carrot, broccoli, or zucchini, sliced chicken breast or minute steak, or a few defrosted prawns –and serve with rice, or noodles. For recipe ideas see pages 174 to 177.

**Egg-fried rice** makes another easy meal using leftover rice from the night before. First make a thin omelet in the bottom of a frying pan, slide out and roll up then fry off some chopped onion and garlic with diced bacon. Add some mixed frozen veg and the rice, stir-fry until the

veg are cooked through and the rice is hot. Flavor with soy sauce, chili sauce or some fish sauce if you have it. Stir in the sliced omelet and warm through.

**Deep dish tortillas**, Spanish omelets or frittatas are thick omelets with lots of bits and pieces added. You can use easily available vegetables, such as onions, scallions, and mushrooms and thrown in leftovers such as sliced potatoes and sliced cooked sausage, or chorizo. Omelets are good served with a simple salad.

**Hash potatoes**, made with diced raw or cooked potatoes fried in oil with chopped onion and garlic can be made into a hearty supper with the addition of sliced mushrooms, diced cooked beet, diced bacon or ham, or even diced corned beef or canned salmon. To make bubble and squeak, add sliced cabbage or kale. To spice up the potatoes, add chili or paprika, if you fancy. Hash potatoes can also be topped with a fried egg.

### canned beans and legumes vs dried
Canned beans are indispensable, especially if cooking for one. If cooking for a crowd use cheaper dried legumes, bearing in mind that most dried pulses need to be soaked overnight. As a general guide if a recipe calls for canned beans and you would like to use dried, use half the weight of the canned beans, but remember that the can also contains water, so in a 13 oz can of beans, the drained weight of beans is around 8 oz (1½ cups).

minutes, stirring all the time for even cooking.

**Pan-fry** To fry foods in a skillet with just 1–2 tablespoons oil.

**Steam** To cook foods in a covered perforated saucepan set over a lower saucepan half-filled with boiling water, so it is not in direct contact with water.

**Simmer** To cook soup, casseroles and sauces over a low heat so bubbles just break the surface.

**Mash** This can be done with a fork, for example, when mashing a banana or avocado on a plate until smooth. Larger amounts of vegetables are best mashed with a larger metal masher or hand-held immersion blender in the saucepan they were cooked in.

**Roux** This is the base of a cheese or white sauce. To make a roux, melt the butter in a saucepan, then stir in the flour until the mixture binds together. Cook briefly, then stir in milk with a wooden spoon until smooth. Continue to stir until the sauce comes to the boil, is a pouring thickness, and hopefully lump free. If there are lumps in your sauce, these can be whisked out with a small balloon whisk.

**Blending** This term is used when making short pastry and in some cakes. Butter is cut in small cubes and added to flour. Dip your hands into this mixture and lift it up, then blend between your fingertips to break up the fat until it resembles bread crumbs.

**Creaming** This term is used when making cakes. Butter or soft margarine is beaten with sugar in a bowl with a wooden spoon or electric mixer, if you have one, until it is creamy smooth and pale in color.

Red, green, and the tiny Puy lentils don't need soaking overnight before you cook them, and couscous only needs only soaking in boiling water for 5 minutes before use. Adding beans, lentils, or root vegetables to meaty casseroles means you can cut down the amount of meat per serving without compromising on portion size.

Breakfast cereals needn't only be eaten for breakfast, they're low in fat and served with milk make a quick healthy any time-of-day snack. Top with some sliced bananas, some diced dried apricots, or a few raisins, or a few fresh berries, if you have them.

## crash course in cooking terms…

**Stir-fry** To cook thinly sliced vegetables and meat or fish in a little oil in a wok or large skillet over a high heat for just a matter of

### get used to your oven

All ovens vary slightly. Fan ovens cook more quickly than those with top and bottom heat. As a general rule, for a fan oven use an oven temperature 10–20° below the temperatures given in the recipes in this book and check on food in the oven 10–15 minutes before the end of cooking to make sure it isn't overcooking. If the food is overbrowning cover the top with foil to stop it burning and lower the oven temperature slightly.

### how can you tell if food is cooked?

Chicken, turkey, and pork must be thoroughly cooked before serving. Even though recipes have cooking times it is always worth double-checking food is cooked through before you serve it up. To test whether meat and poultry is cooked, insert a skewer or thin-bladed knife into the thickest part of the meat. For a whole chicken or turkey, skewer through the thickest part of the drumstick into the breast meat, then wait for a few seconds – if the juices run clear it is ready, if there are any traces of pink, indicating blood is still present then it needs a little longer. Cook for 10 minutes more then test again. For pork chops or a joint insert the skewer into the center then check the meat juices in the same way.

Beef and lamb can be eaten slightly pink, according to taste.

Fish is cooked through when it is the same color all the way through and the flesh breaks easily into flakes. Uncooked shrimp will turn

pink all over when cooked through. Fresh tuna is the only exception and like beef steak can be eaten rare.

When cooked, pasta and rice should be tender with a little bite – for pasta this is called al dente. To check, take a little out of the pan, cool, then taste. The same goes for vegetables – take a small piece out the pan and eat when cool enough, but remember that the large pieces will take longer to cook, so test these with a knife: if it goes in easily they are tender.

To check if a cake is cooked, don't open the oven for the first 20 minutes or the cake will sink; check at regular intervals after this time so it doesn't burn. Press the top of a shallow sandwich-style cake with your fingertip; if it feels firm or springs back then it is ready. For deeper cakes, press a wooden skewer or small knife into the centre; if it comes out clean the cake is ready, if it is smeared with mixture cook a little longer and then check again. Cover the top of the cake with foil if it seems to be browning too quickly.

When reheating food that has been defrosted from frozen, only do this once and make sure that the food is boiling hot right through to the center when you reheat it.

## improvising

The following tips show how resourcefulness can be all-important when it comes to cookery.

**Don't have a rolling pin?** Try using a washed beer glass or cordial bottle, or even a washed full can of soda.

**Need a cookie cutter?** Use an upturned, clean glass and cut around the rim with a small knife.
**To make bread crumbs without a blender,** grate the crust, bread, or bread roll on the coarse section of a grater. The bread needs to be in one chunk, sliced bread will mean fingers get grated too.

**Want to steam some veg but don't have a special steamer pan,** then put the veg into a large metal strainer or colander and set this over a saucepan half-filled with boiling water making sure that the water is well below the strainer or colander. Cover with a large lid and cook until the veg are just tender.

**Short of pans or oven space?** Rice noodles don't need cooking in the same way as wheat

pasta but can be soaked in a bowl of boiling water for 3–5 minutes until soft and hot, then drained and added to stir-fries.

**Don't have quite the right pan?** Use what you do have – metal saucepans with metal handles can be used on the burner and in the oven: china or pottery casserole dishes can only be used in the oven, so fry off meat and veggies in a skillet, add the stock and bring to a boil then transfer to the casserole and finish off in the oven.

**Cake pan is bigger than you need?** Reduce the recipe cooking time as the cake will be thinner and therefore cook more quickly. Increase the cooking time if the pan is smaller than required, as the cake will be deeper and so take longer to cook.

## do's and don'ts

• Metal things can't be used in a microwave. This includes metallic trims on glass or china. Some china gets hot in the microwave, this tends to be the thicker, chunkier kind.
• Keep dairy and meat items separately, and raw and cooked meat apart in the refrigerator. Cover food so that it doesn't dry out.
• Check dates on bought food. Sell-by dates are the dates food must be sold by in the shops; use-by dates, the date it must be eaten by at home. Throw food away after that date.
• Cook frozen veggies and fruit from frozen.
• Meat and fish must be defrosted thoroughly before cooking.
• If you only need one portion reheated take it

out of the larger dish transfer to a smaller dish to heat up and put the rest back in the fridge.
• Do not put defrosted food back in the freezer in its raw state. It must be cooked, cooled, and then put back into the freezer.
• To speed up defrosting, put frozen food in cold water and change the water several times.

# soups, stews, & casseroles

# pork & red pepper chili

Serves **4**
Preparation time **10 minutes**
Cooking time **30 minutes**

2 tablespoons **olive oil**
1 large **onion**, chopped
1 **red bell pepper**, cored,
   seeded, and diced
2 **garlic cloves**, crushed
1 lb **ground pork**
1 **fresh red chili**, seeded and
   finely chopped
1 teaspoon **dried oregano**
2 cups **pureed tomatoes**
13 oz can **red kidney beans**,
   drained and rinsed
**salt** and **pepper**
**basil leaves**, to garnish
**sour cream**, to serve

**Heat** the oil in a saucepan over a medium heat. Add the onion and bell pepper and cook for 5 minutes until soft and starting to brown, then add the garlic and cook for another 30 seconds or so. Next, add the ground pork and cook, stirring and breaking up the meat with a wooden spoon, for 5 minutes or until browned.

**Add** the remaining ingredients, except the sour cream, and bring to a boil. Reduce the heat and simmer gently for 20 minutes. Remove from the heat, season well with salt and pepper, and garnish with sour cream and basil leaves. Serve with boiled rice or crusty bread on the side.

**For lamb & eggplant chili**, replace the bell pepper with 1 medium eggplant, cut into small cubes. Fry as above with the onion and garlic, then add 1 lb ground lamb instead of the pork. Continue as above. Sprinkle the finished dish with 2 tablespoons finely chopped mint leaves, omitting the sour cream, and serve with rice or pasta.

# vietnamese beef pho

Serves **6**
Preparation time **15 minutes**
Cooking time **20 minutes**

6 cups good-quality
  **chicken stock**
2 **lemon grass stalks**, bruised
small piece of **fresh ginger
  root**, peeled and
  thinly sliced
2 tablespoons **light soy sauce**
2 tablespoons **lime juice**
2 teaspoons **dark
  brown sugar**
4 oz **dried flat rice noodles**
9 oz **sirloin steak**, sliced

**To serve**
1½ cups **bean sprouts**
1 **fresh red chili**, seeded and
  thinly sliced
handful of **Thai basil**
handful of **mint**

**Put** the stock, lemon grass, ginger, soy sauce, lime, juice and sugar in a large heavy saucepan and bring to a boil. Reduce the heat and simmer gently for 10 minutes until fragrant.

**Remove** the lemon grass and ginger using a slotted spoon; discard. Add the rice noodles to the simmering broth and cook according to the pack instructions, adding the sliced steak for the last 2–3 minutes of the cooking time to cook through.

**Spoon** into warm soup bowls, top with the bean sprouts, chili, basil, and mint and serve immediately.

**For salmon pho**, cook the stock using fish stock insteaad of chicken stock. Dice 8 oz skinned and pin-boned salmon (or trout) fillets, add to the fragrant stock after removing the lemon grass and ginger, and simmer for 6–8 minutes until the fish is just cooked through. Meanwhile, cook the rice noodles separately in boiling water for 2–3 minutes. Drain and divide among 6 warm soup bowls, then spoon over the broth. Top with the bean sprouts, chili and herbs, and serve immediately.

# gruyère, bacon, & potato soup

Serves **6**
Preparation time **20 minutes**
Cooking time **30 minutes**

2 tablespoons **olive oil**
3 **rindless bacon slices,**
   chopped
2 **onions**, finely chopped
2½ cups good-quality
   **chicken stock**
3½ cups **water**
1¼ lb **potatoes**, peeled and
   cut into ½ inch cubes
¼ cup **all-purpose flour**
2 oz **Gruyère cheese**, grated
1 tablespoon **medium-
   dry sherry**
1 teaspoon **Worcestershire
   sauce**
3 tablespoons finely chopped
   **flat-leaf parsley** (optional)
**salt** and **pepper**

**Put** the oil in a large heavy saucepan over a medium heat. Add the bacon and onions and cook for about 5 minutes until the onion is soft and pale golden.

**Pour** in the stock and 2½ cups of the measurement water, add the potatoes, and bring to a boil. Reduce the heat, cover, and simmer for about 15 minutes until the potatoes are tender.

**Whisk** the flour with the remaining measurement water in a small bowl then stir the mixture into the soup. Cover and simmer, stirring frequently, for another 5 minutes.

**Blend** the Gruyère with 1¼ cups of the soup in a blender or food processor until smooth. Return to the pan and add the sherry and Worcestershire sauce. Season with salt and pepper, bearing in mind the saltiness of the bacon and cheese. Gently simmer for 3–5 minutes.

**Stir** in the parsley, if using, and serve immediately in warm soup bowls with broiled cheese on toast sprinkled with a little Worcestershire sauce, if desired.

**For celeriac soup with bacon & blue cheese**, fry the bacon and onions in the oil as above. Add the stock, measurement water, and 1¼ lb peeled and diced celeriac instead of the potatoes. Continue as above, adding 2 oz blue cheese such as Stilton or Danish blue, rind removed and diced, instead of the Gruyère. Puree the soup until smooth, then return to the pan to heat through, omitting the sherry and Worcestershire sauce. Garnish with the parsley and some extra diced cheese.

# jamaican pepperpot soup

Serves **6**
Preparation time **20 minutes**
Cooking time **1 hour**
**10 minutes**

2 lb **lean stewing beef**, cut
into cubes
8 oz **boneless lean pork**, cut
into cubes
2½ quarts **water**
24 **okra**, trimmed and
chopped
1 lb **kale**, tough stalks
discarded, roughly chopped
2 **green bell peppers**, cored,
seeded, and chopped
2 **scallions**, roughly chopped
sprig of **thyme**
¼ teaspoon **cayenne pepper**
1 lb **yellow yams**, peeled
and diced
2 small **potatoes**, peeled
and sliced
1 **garlic clove**, finely chopped
**salt**

**Put** the meat and measurement water in a large saucepan. Bring to a boil, then reduce the heat, partially cover, and simmer for about 30 minutes.

**Add** the okra, kale, green peppers, and scallions to the soup with the thyme and cayenne pepper. Partially cover and simmer over a medium heat for 15 minutes.

**Tip** in the yams, potatoes, and garlic and simmer for another 20 minutes or until the yams and potato are tender and the meat is cooked through. Add more water if the soup is too thick. Season with salt and serve in warm soup bowls with crusty bread, if desired.

**For extra hot pepperpot soup with dumplings**, add a 3 inch piece of fresh ginger root, finely chopped, and 2 seeded and finely chopped Scotch bonnet chilies instead of the cayenne pepper. While the yams cook, mix 1¼ cups all-purpose flour with a little salt and 4–5 tablespoons water to make the dumpling dough; it should be soft and slightly sticky. Rub your hands with a little vegetable oil, then divide the dough into 24 pieces, shape into ovals, and carefully drop the dumplings into the soup. Cover the pan again and cook for about 10 minutes.

# meat tortellini in brodo

Serves **4**
Preparation time **5 minutes**
Cooking time **20 minutes**

8 sheets **fresh lasagne sheets**
**semola di grano duro**
   **(coarse semolina)** for dusting
2½ cups good-quality **beef or**
   **chicken stock**, boiling
2 **tomatoes**, diced
handful of **basil leaves**
**salt** and **pepper**
freshly grated **Parmesan**
   **cheese**, to serve

**Filling**
1 teaspoon **olive oil**
1 small **onion**, finely chopped
1 **garlic clove**, finely chopped
7 oz **ground pork**
2 oz **prosciutto crudo**,
   roughly chopped
1 tablespoon chopped **flat-**
   **leaf parsley**
4 tablespoons **dry white wine**
2 tablespoons freshly grated
   **Parmesan cheese**
2 tablespoons **dried bread**
   **crumbs**
¼ teaspoon freshly grated
   **nutmeg**

**Make** the filling first. Heat the oil in a heavy skillet over a low heat. Add the onion and garlic. Cook, stirring frequently, for 6–7 minutes until soft and translucent. Add the meat and prosciutto, and cook over a medium heat, breaking up and stirring frequently, for 10 minutes until the meat is cooked. Add the parsley and wine and cook until the liquid has evaporated. Cool and transfer to a food processor or blender with the remaining filling ingredients. Season and blend to a coarse paste.

**Cut** the lasagne sheets into 3½ inch squares and place a nutmeg-size ball of filling in the center of each square. Brush a little water around the edges of the squares, then fold the dough over the filling to make triangles. Gently but firmly push down around the filling, sealing the pasta and ensuring that no air has been trapped. Bring the corners on the longest edge of the triangles together, and pinch tightly to seal. Set aside on a baking sheet lightly dusted with semola di grano duro, and cover with a clean dish towel.

**Put** the stock in a large saucepan, and season with a little salt. Add the tortellini, diced tomatoes, and basil, and cook for 2–3 minutes until al dente. Serve the tortellini in warm bowls with the broth, sprinkled with grated Parmesan.

**For speedy spinach tortellini in brodo**, heat 4 cups good-quality chicken stock in a large saucepan. Add 2 x 10 oz packages ready-made chilled spinach-stuffed tortellini. Cook as above, omitting the tomatoes and basil. Add 5 oz fresh spinach and 2 tablespoons lemon juice, season with salt and pepper, and cook for another 1 minute until the spinach just wilts. Serve with freshly grated Parmesan cheese.

# white bean soup provençal

Serves **6**

Preparation time **15 minutes**, plus soaking

Cooking time **1¼–1¾ hours**

3 tablespoons **olive oil**

2 **garlic cloves**, crushed

1 small **red bell pepper**, cored, seeded, and chopped

1 **onion**, finely chopped

8 oz **tomatoes**, finely chopped

1 teaspoon finely chopped **thyme**

½ cup **dried navy** or **cannellini beans**, soaked overnight in cold water, rinsed, and drained

2½ cups **water**

2½ cups **vegetable stock**

2 tablespoons finely chopped **flat-leaf parsley**

**salt** and **pepper**

**Heat** the oil in a large heavy saucepan, add the garlic, red pepper, and onion and cook over a medium heat for 5 minutes or until softened.

**Add** the tomatoes and thyme and cook for 1 minute. Add the beans and pour in the measurement water and stock. Bring to a boil, then reduce the heat, cover, and simmer for 1–1½ hours until the beans are tender (you may need to allow for a longer cooking time, depending on how old the beans are).

**Sprinkle** in the parsley and season with salt and pepper. Serve immediately in warm soup bowls with fresh, crusty bread.

**For Spanish white bean soup**, add 14 oz diced chorizo sausage when frying the onions, garlic, and red pepper. Stir in 1 teaspoon pimentón (Spanish smoked paprika) or 1 teaspoon mild chili powder. Cook for 1 minute until fragrant, then add the tomatoes and continue the recipe as above.

# quick sausage & bean casserole

Serves **4**
Preparation time **5 minutes**
Cooking time **25 minutes**

2 tablespoons **olive oil**
16 **baby pork sausages**,
  separated
2 **garlic cloves**, crushed
13 oz can **chopped tomatoes**
13 oz can **baked beans**
7 oz can **mixed beans**,
  drained and rinsed
½ teaspoon **dried thyme**
**salt** and **pepper**
3 tablespoons chopped **flat-
  leaf parsley** (optional),
  to garnish

**Heat** the oil in a skillet over a medium-high heat. Add the sausages and cook for a few minutes until nicely browned all over.

**Transfer** the sausages to a large saucepan and add the remaining ingredients except the parsley. Bring to a boil, then reduce the heat, cover tightly, and simmer for 20 minutes until the sausages are cooked through.

**Season** with salt and pepper, sprinkle with the parsley, if using, and serve hot with mustard mash (see below).

**For mustard mash**, to serve as an accompaniment, cook 2 lb chopped floury potatoes in a large saucepan of salted boiling water until tender; be careful not to overcook, or the potatoes will become waterlogged. Drain well and return to the pan. Mash with ¹/₃ cup butter, 1 tablespoon whole grain mustard, 3 teaspoons English mustard, and 1 crushed garlic clove. Season with salt and pepper, then beat in 2 tablespoons chopped flat-leaf parsley and a dash of olive oil. Serve hot with the casserole.

# spanish chickpea soup

Serves **8**
Preparation time **15 minutes**,
  plus soaking
Cooking time **2¼ hours**

1 cup **dried chickpeas**,
  soaked for 48 hours in
  cold water or 12 hours in
  boiling water
1–1½ lb **boneless smoked
  bacon hock joint**
1 **onion**, studded with
  4 **cloves**
2 **garlic cloves,** crushed
1 **bay leaf**
sprig of **thyme**
sprig of **marjoram**
sprig of **flat-leaf parsley**
7 cups **water**
7 cups **chicken stock**
10–12 oz **potatoes**, cut into
  ½ inch cubes
3 cups **Savoy cabbage**,
  shredded
**salt** and **pepper**

**Drain** the chickpeas, rinse under cold running water, and drain again. Put the bacon joint in a large, deep saucepan and cover with cold water. Bring the water briefly to a boil, then drain, discarding the water.

**Transfer** the bacon joint to a clean, large heavy saucepan. Add the chickpeas, studded onion, garlic, bay leaf, thyme, marjoram, parsley, and measurement water. Bring to a boil, then reduce the heat, partially cover, and simmer for 1½ hours until the meat is tender.

**Remove** and discard the onion and herbs. Remove the hock, transfer to a board, and cut into small pieces. Set aside. Add the stock, potatoes, and cabbage to the pan, and simmer for 30 minutes more.

**Add** the reserved hock pieces to the soup and cook for an additional 10 minutes. Season with salt and pepper. Ladle the soup into warm soup bowls and serve with fresh, crusty bread.

**For mixed pea & bacon soup**, replace the chickpeas with 1 cup country soup mix (a blend of dried yellow and green split peas, pearl barley, and red lentils). Put the country soup mix in a strainer, pick over for any grit or damaged lentils, and rinse under cold running water. Drain and add to the pan with the bacon joint; bring to a boil, then drain. Transfer to a clean pan and add the clove-studded onion, 2 bay leaves, 2 teaspoons English mustard, and the measurement water. Continue as above. Add the stock, potatoes, and 2 diced carrots, omitting the cabbage. Finish the soup as above.

# noodle soup with shrimp tempura

Serves **5**
Preparation time **20 minutes**
Cooking time **15 minutes**

4 oz **dried soba noodles**
2 teaspoons **sesame oil**
1 bunch of **scallions**, sliced
2 **bok choy**, shredded
7 cups **hot vegetable stock**
4 tablespoons **sake**
2 tablespoons **dark soy sauce**
1 cup **bean sprouts**
**vegetable oil**, for deep-frying
12 **raw jumbo shrimp**,
    thawed if frozen, peeled,
    and deveined
2 sheets of **nori**, shredded
    (optional)

**Tempura batter**
1 **egg yolk**
½ cup **all-purpose flour**
6 tablespoons **ice water**

**Cook** the soba noodles according to the package instructions. Rinse in a colander under hot running water. Drain well.

**Heat** the sesame oil in a large wok. Add the scallions and bok choy, and stir-fry over medium-high heat for 1 minute. Pour in the stock, sake, and soy sauce and simmer gently for 5 minutes. Stir in the bean sprouts.

**Make** the tempura while the stir-fry is simmering. In a bowl, briefly whisk together the egg yolk, flour, and water to make a slightly lumpy batter. Heat the vegetable oil in a separate wok, a deep heavy saucepan or a deep-fat fryer to 350°–375°F, or until a cube of bread dropped into the oil browns in 30 seconds. Dip the shrimp in the batter, then carefully drop them into the hot oil and cook for 3 minutes or until the shrimp have turned pink and the batter is golden. Remove with a slotted spoon and drain on paper towels.

**Spoon** the noodles into warm soup bowls, add the soup, and top with the shrimp and strips of nori, if desired. Serve immediately.

**For noodle soup with black beans**, make up the noodles and soup as above, but omit the shrimp tempura. Add ½ cup black bean sauce or stir-fry sauce and ½–1 seeded and sliced small fresh red chili with the stock, sake, and soy sauce. Simmer the soup for 5 minutes, then add the bean sprouts. Serve immediately, sprinkled with chopped peanuts instead of the shrimp and nori topping.

# goulash soup

Serves **6**
Preparation time **15 minutes**
Cooking time 1¼ **hours**

3 tablespoons **vegetable oil**
1½ lb **boneless**
  **lean beef**, cut into
  1 inch strips
2 **onions**, chopped
2 **garlic cloves**, crushed
2 **celery sticks**, sliced
3 tablespoons **paprika**
1 tablespoon **caraway seeds**
5 cups **beef stock**
2½ cups **water**
¼ teaspoon **dried thyme**
**2 bay leaves**
¼ teaspoon **Tabasco sauce**
  (or to taste)
3 tablespoons **tomato paste**
8 oz **potatoes**, peeled and cut
  into ½ inch cubes
3 **carrots**, cut into ½ inch
  cubes
**sour cream**, to serve
  (optional)

**Put** the oil in a large heavy saucepan over a medium-high heat. When the oil is hot, add the beef, in batches to avoid crowding the pan, and cook for a few minutes until browned all over. As each batch browns, remove with a slotted spoon and drain on paper. towels. Reduce the heat to medium and add the onions, garlic, and celery to the pan. Cook for 5 minutes or until softened.

**Remove** from the heat and stir in the paprika and caraway seeds. Pour in the stock and measurement water. Add the thyme, bay leaves, Tabasco sauce, and tomato paste. Stir well and add the browned beef. Bring to a boil, then reduce the heat, partially cover, and simmer for about 30 minutes.

**Add** the potatoes and carrots and simmer for another 30 minutes or until the beef and potatoes are tender. Remove and discard the bay leaves. Spoon the soup into warm soup bowls, garnish each portion with a dollop of sour cream, if desired, and serve immediately.

**For goulash soup with white fish**, make up the soup as above, omitting the beef and using 5 cups fish stock instead of the beef stock and measurement water. Simmer for 30 minutes, then add 1 lb skinned haddock or cod fillet. Simmer gently for another 10 minutes, then lift out the fish and break into pieces. Remove any bones, then return the fish to the soup. Serve with sour cream, sprinkled with a little chopped dill weed or flat- leaf parsley.

# chicken stew with dumplings

Serves **4**
Preparation time **30 minutes**
Cooking time **1½ hours**

8 **boneless, skinless chicken
  thighs**, halved
1 tablespoon **sunflower oil**
1 **onion**, roughly chopped
2 **parsnips**, cut into chunks
2 **carrots**, cut into chunks
6 oz **rutabaga**, cut into chunks
¼ cup **pearl barley**
12 fl oz bottle **English beer**
1¼ cups **chicken stock**
2 teaspoons **English mustard**
**salt** and **pepper**

**Dumplings**
1½ cups **self-rising flour**
½ cup **light shredded suet**
4 tablespoons chopped
  **chives**
6–8 tablespoons **cold water**

**Put** the oil in a flameproof casserole over a high heat. When the oil is hot, add the chicken and onion, and fry for about 5 minutes until golden.

**Stir** in the remaining vegetables and cook for 2 minutes until starting to soften, then mix in the pearl barley, beer, stock, and mustard. Season with salt and pepper and bring to a boil. Cover and transfer to a preheated oven, 350°F, for 1 hour.

**Make** the dumplings almost at the end of the chicken stew's cooking time. Mix together the flour, suet, and chives in a bowl and season with a little salt and pepper. Stir in enough of the measurement water, adding a little at a time, to mix to a soft, slightly sticky dough. Shape dessertspoons of the mixture into balls.

**Remove** the chicken stew from the oven, transfer to the stovetop, and stir through. When the stock is boiling, carefully add the dumplings so that they sit on the surface, leaving space around each one. Cover and simmer for about 15 minutes until the dumplings are light and fluffy and the chicken is cooked through. (Keeping the lid on while cooking makes the dumplings rise well.) Spoon into warm shallow bowls to serve.

**For chicken hotpot**, omit the dumplings and cover the top of the stew with 1¼ lb peeled and thinly sliced potatoes arranged in an overlapping layer before it goes into the oven. Cover and cook for 1 hour. Remove the lid, dot the potatoes with 2 tablespoons butter, season with salt and pepper, and cook for another 30 minutes until the potatoes are lightly browned and the chicken is cooked through.

# spiced lamb & sweet potato soup

Serves **6**
Preparation time **30 minutes**
Cooking time **2¾–3 hours**

1 tablespoon **olive oil**
1 lb **stewing lamb on the bone**
1 **onion**, finely chopped
1–2 **garlic cloves**, finely chopped
1 inch piece of **fresh ginger root**, grated
2 teaspoons **ras el hanout** (Moroccan spice blend)
8 cups **lamb** or **chicken stock**
6 tablespoons **red lentils**, picked over, rinsed and drained
10 oz **sweet potatoes**, peeled and diced
1 cup diced **carrots**
**salt** and **pepper**
small bunch of **fresh cilantro**, to garnish (optional)

**Heat** the oil in a large heavy saucepan over a medium-high heat. When the oil is hot, add the lamb and fry for a couple of minutes until browned on one side. Reduce the heat slightly, turn the meat over, and add the onion. Continue cooking until the lamb is browned all over and the onion is softened and starting to brown.

**Stir** in the garlic, ginger, and ras el hanout. Cook, stirring, for about 30 seconds until fragrant, then add the stock and lentils and season. Bring to a boil, reduce the heat, cover, and simmer for 1½ hours.

**Add** the sweet potatoes and carrots, bring back to a simmer, then cover the pan again and simmer the soup gently for 1 hour. Lift the lamb out of the soup with a slotted spoon, transfer to a plate, and carefully remove the bones and any excess fat, breaking the meat into small pieces. Return the meat to the pan and heat through. Taste and adjust the seasoning if desired. Ladle the soup into bowls, sprinkle with torn cilantro leaves, and serve with hot flat breads.

**For homemade fennel flat breads**, to serve as an accompaniment, put 1¾ cups self-rising flour and ½ teaspoon baking powder in a bowl. Using a mortar and pestle, crush 1 teaspoon fennel seeds. Add the crushed seeds to the flour and season with salt and pepper. Stir. Add 2 tablespoons olive oil, then gradually mix in 6 tablespoons water, a little at a time, using just enough to make a soft dough. Cut the dough into 6 pieces, then roll out each piece on a lightly floured surface into a rough oval shape about the size of a hand. Cook on a preheated griddle pan or heavy skillet for 3–4 minutes each side until singed and puffy.

# quick one-pot ratatouille

Serves **4**

Preparation time **10 minutes**

Cooking time **20 minutes**

6 tablespoons **olive oil**

2 **onions**, chopped

1 **eggplant**, cut into bite-size
cubes

2 large **zucchini**, cut into bite-
size pieces

1 **red bell pepper**, cored,
seeded, and cut into bite-
size pieces

1 **yellow bell pepper**, cored,
seeded, and cut into bite-
size pieces

2 **garlic cloves**, crushed

13 oz can **chopped tomatoes**

4 tablespoons chopped
**parsley** or **basil**

**salt** and **pepper**

**Heat** the oil in a large saucepan until very hot. Add the
onions, eggplant, zucchini, red and yellow bell peppers,
and garlic, and cook, stirring constantly, for a few
minutes until softened. Add the tomatoes, season
with salt and pepper, and stir well.

**Reduce** the heat, cover the pan tightly, and simmer for
15 minutes until all the vegetables are cooked. Remove
from the heat and stir in the chopped parsley or basil
before serving.

**For Mediterranean vegetable pie**, spoon the cooked
vegetable mixture into a medium-sized ovenproof dish.
Cook 1 lb 10 oz peeled and quartered floury potatoes
in a large saucepan of salted boiling water for 12–15
minutes until tender. Drain and roughly mash with
2 cups finely grated cheddar cheese. Spread over the
vegetable mixture, then bake in a preheated oven,
350°F, for 20 minutes or until lightly golden on top.

# steak & ale casserole

Serves **5–6**
Preparation time **20 minutes**
Cooking time 1¾ **hours**

2 tablespoons **all-
    purpose flour**
2 lb **braising steak**,
    cut into chunks
2 tablespoons **butter**
1 tablespoon **vegetable oil**
2 **onions**, chopped
2 **celery sticks**, sliced
a few **sprigs** of **thyme**
2 **bay leaves**
1²/₃ cups **English beer**
1¼ cups **beef stock**
2 tablespoons **molasses**
1 lb **parsnips**, peeled and cut
    into wedges
**salt** and **pepper**

**Season** the flour with salt and pepper and use to coat the beef. Melt the butter with the oil in a large flameproof casserole over a medium-high heat. Working in batches to avoid crowding the casserole, fry the beef for a few minutes until well browned all over. As each batch browns, remove with a slotted spoon and set aside on a plate.

**Put** the onions and celery in the casserole and fry gently for 5 minutes until soft and translucent. Return the beef to the pan and add the herbs, beer, stock, and molasses. Stir through. Bring just to a boil, then reduce the heat and cover. Bake in a preheated oven, 325°F, for 1 hour.

**Add** the parsnips to the casserole, cover again, and return to the oven for another 30 minutes or until the beef and parsnips are tender. Check the seasoning and serve.

**For Irish champ**, to serve as an accompaniment, cook 3 lb scrubbed floury potatoes in a large saucepan of salted boiling water for 20 minutes. Peel away the skins, then return to the pan and mash. Beat in ²/₃ cup milk, 3–4 finely chopped scallions, and ¼ cup butter. Season with salt and pepper. Serve hot.

# simple
# suppers

# pasta with tomato & basil sauce

Serves **4**
Preparation time **10 minutes**
Cooking time **10 minutes**

13 oz **dried spaghetti**
5 tablespoons **olive oil**
5 **garlic cloves**, finely chopped
6 **vine-ripened tomatoes**,
   seeded and chopped
½ cup **basil leaves**
**salt** and **pepper**

**Cook** the pasta in a large saucepan of salted boiling water according to the package instructions until al dente.

**Heat** half the oil while the pasta is cooking in a skillet over a low heat. Add the garlic and cook for 1 minute. As soon as the garlic begins to change color, remove the pan from the heat and add the remaining oil.

**Drain** the pasta and return to the pan. Add the garlic-infused oil with the chopped tomatoes and basil leaves. Season and toss well to mix. Serve immediately.

**For quick tomato & basil pizza**, prepare the garlic-infused oil as above, but use 4 tablespoons olive oil and 4 finely chopped garlic cloves. Meanwhile, skin the tomatoes and seed and chop as above. Pour off half the oil and reserve, add the tomatoes and half the basil to the pan, season well with salt and pepper, and allow to simmer while you make the dough. Sift 2 cups self-rising flour and 1 teaspoon salt into a large bowl, then gradually add ²/₃ cup warm water, mixing well to form a soft dough. Work the dough into a ball with your hands. Knead on a lightly floured surface until smooth and soft. Roll out the dough to a 12 inch round, making a border around the edge slightly thicker than the center, and lay on a warmed baking sheet. Spread the tomato mixture over the dough base, top with 4 oz sliced mozzarella cheese, and drizzle with the remaining garlic oil. Bake in a preheated oven, 475°F, for 15 minutes or until the base is golden. Sprinkle with the remaining basil leaves and serve immediately.

# thai sesame chicken patties

Serves **4**

Preparation time **15 minutes**, plus chilling

Cooking time **10 minutes**

4 **scallions**

1 cup **fresh cilantro**, plus extra to garnish

1 lb **ground chicken**

3 tablespoons **sesame seeds**, toasted

1 tablespoon **light soy sauce**

1½ inch piece of **fresh ginger root**, peeled and finely grated

1 **egg white**

1 tablespoon **sesame oil**

1 tablespoon **sunflower oil**

**Thai sweet chili dipping sauce**, to serve

**scallion curls**, to garnish (optional)

**Chop** the scallions and cilantro finely in a food processor or with a knife. Put in a bowl and mix with the chicken, sesame seeds, soy sauce, ginger, and egg white.

**Divide** the mixture into 20 mounds on a cutting board, then shape into slightly flattened rounds with wetted hands. Chill in the refrigerator for 1 hour (or longer if you have time).

**Heat** the sesame and sunflower oils in a large skillet, add the patties, and fry for 10 minutes, turning once or twice, until golden and cooked through to the center.

**Arrange** on a serving plate with a small bowl of chili dipping sauce in the centre. Garnish with extra cilantro leaves and spring onion curls, if liked.

**For baby leaf stir-fry with chili**, to serve as an accompaniment, heat 2 teaspoons sesame oil in the same pan used to cook the patties. Add 5 cups ready-prepared baby leaf and baby vegetable stir-fry ingredients and stir-fry for 2–3 minutes until the vegetables are hot. Mix in 2 tablespoons light soy sauce and 1 tablespoon Thai sweet chili dipping sauce. Serve in a side bowl with the chicken patties.

# cod with roasted tomato toast

Serves **4**
Preparation time **15 minutes**
Cooking time **1¼ hours**

4 ripe **tomatoes**, halved
a few sprigs of **thyme**
2 tablespoons **olive oil**
4 **cod fillets**, about 7 oz each,
    skin on and pin-boned
4 slices of **ciabatta**
1 **garlic clove**
**salt** and **pepper**
**Parmesan cheese** shavings,
    to garnish (optional)

**Dressing**
large handful of **basil**
4 tablespoons **olive oil**
2 tablespoons freshly grated
    **Parmesan cheese**

**Arrange** the tomato halves on a baking sheet, season with salt and pepper, sprinkle with the thyme, and drizzle with 1 tablespoon of the oil. Roast in a preheated oven, 325°F, for 1 hour until soft, then increase the oven temperature to 350°F.

**Season** the cod, toward the end of the tomatoes' cooking time, and roast the cod with salt and pepper along with the tomatoes in the oven for 10–12 minutes until the fish is cooked and the tomatoes have softened.

**Brush** both sides of the bread with the remaining oil. Preheat a ridged griddle pan and griddle the bread until golden brown on both sides. Then rub both sides with the garlic clove.

**Put** the ingredients for the dressing in a small food processor and blend until smooth. You can also do this using an immersion blender.

**Top** the toast with the tomatoes, then serve with the cod. Drizzle a little of the dressing over the top and garnish with some Parmesan shavings, if desired.

**For roasted cod & tomato pasta**, while the tomatoes and cod are roasting as above, cook 10 oz dried pasta according to the package instructions until al dente, then drain. Cut the roasted tomatoes into small pieces and flake the cod. Stir through the warm pasta with some of the dressing, prepared as above.

# indonesian-style curry

Serves **4–6**
Preparation time **30 minutes**
Cooking time **4½ hours**

3 tablespoons **coconut** or **vegetable oil**
1½ lb **braising beef**, sliced
3 cups **coconut milk**
1 cup **water**
1 tablespoon **palm sugar** or **brown sugar**
4 **kaffir lime leaves**, shredded
3 **star anise**
1 large **cinnamon stick**
½ teaspoon **salt**

**Spice paste**
1 teaspoon each **salt** and **ground turmeric**
½ teaspoon **chili powder**
6 **garlic cloves**, chopped
2 inch piece each of **fresh ginger root**, peeled and grated and **galangal**, peeled and grated
1 teaspoon **black peppercorns**, crushed
4 **cardamom pods**, bruised
4 **fresh red chilies**, chopped
1 **lemon grass stalk**, tough outer layers removed, chopped
3 large **onions**, chopped
1 tablespoon **tamarind paste**

**Process** the spice paste ingredients up to and including the chilies in a blender or food processor until roughly chopped, or pound using a mortar and pestle. Add the lemon grass and onions, and process or pound to a dry paste. Add the tamarind paste and blend together.

**Heat** the oil in a large saucepan over a medium-high heat. Working in batches, fry the beef for a few minutes until browned on all sides. Remove each batch with a slotted spoon and set aside on a plate. Add the spice paste to the hot pan, and fry for 2–3 minutes, stirring constantly. Return the reserved beef to the pan with all the remaining ingredients, reduce the heat slightly and bring slowly to a boil, stirring constantly.

**Reduce** the heat again to as low as possible, and simmer very gently for 4–4½ hours, stirring occasionally, until the meat is tender and the sauce has reduced and thickened—the flavor improves with slow cooking.

**Increase** the heat when the sauce is very thick to make a true 'dry' rendang, if desired. Stirring constantly, fry the beef in the thick sauce until it is a rich brown color and almost dry, and nearly all of the sauce has been absorbed. Serve hot.

**For egg rendang**, omit the beef from the recipe and fry 1 roughly chopped onion and 2 potatoes, cut into large dice, for 5 minutes instead. Add the spice paste and remaining ingredients. Simmer for 1 hour, then remove the potatoes and set aside. Continue cooking until the sauce has reduced and thickened. Return the potatoes to the pan with 6 hard-cooked eggs, peeled and halved, and cook for 5 minutes to heat through.

# eggplant, basil, & ricotta pizza

Serves **4**

Preparation time **10 minutes**

Cooking time **50 minutes**

²/₃ cup **pureed tomatoes**

5 large **basil leaves**, torn, plus
extra leaves, to garnish

1 **garlic clove**, crushed

2–3 small–medium **eggplants**,
cut lengthwise into ¼ inch
thick slices

4 fresh **pizza bases**

½ cup **ricotta cheese**, broken
into small chunks

3 oz **mozzarella cheese**
(drained weight), roughly
chopped

**olive oil** for glazing

**salt**

**Combine** the pureed tomatoes, torn basil leaves, and garlic in a bowl. Season lightly with salt, cover, and allow to infuse while you cook the eggplants.

**Heat** a ridged griddle pan over a high heat until smoking hot. Add the eggplants, in batches, and cook for 2 minutes on each side until charred on the outside and soft all the way through.

**Put** a baking sheet in a preheated oven, 475°F, to heat through. Place 1 pizza base on the base only of a well-floured 9 inch removable tart pan.

**Spoon** 2 tablespoons of the tomato mixture over the base, top with a quarter of the eggplants, then sprinkle with a quarter each of the cheeses. Brush the border with oil, to glaze. Remove the heated baking sheet from the oven, slide the pan onto it, then quickly return to the oven. Bake for 7–8 minutes until crisp and risen. Serve immediately, garnished with basil leaves. As the first pizza cooks, prepare the next for the oven.

**For zucchini & smoked mozzarella pizza**, replace the eggplants with 4 zucchinis, cut lengthwise into ¼ inch thick slices, and griddle as above. Omit the ricotta and mozzarella cheeses, and replace with 5 oz sliced smoked mozzarella or caciocavallo cheese.

# chicken teriyaki

Serves **4**
Preparation time **10 minutes**
Cooking time **10 minutes**

1 ¼ lb **boneless, skinless chicken breasts**, cubed
about 8 **scallions**, cut into 2 inch lengths, plus 1 extra, finely chopped, to garnish
2 **red bell peppers**, cored, seeded, and cut into chunks
2 tablespoons **vegetable oil**

**Teriyaki sauce**
3 tablespoons **Japanese soy sauce** or **Chinese dark soy sauce**
3 tablespoons **runny honey**
3 tablespoons **sake** or **dry sherry**
1 **garlic clove**, crushed
3 slices of peeled **fresh ginger root**

**Put** all the sauce ingredients into a small saucepan, and simmer for 5 minutes until thickened.

**Meanwhile,** divide the chicken cubes, scallion lengths, and red peppers evenly among 8 metal skewers, threading the ingredients alternately. Brush with oil.

**Heat** a ridged griddle pan until hot. Arrange the chicken skewers in the pan and cook for 4 minutes on each side or until cooked through. Alternatively, cook under a preheated very hot broiler.

**Brush** the skewers with the teriyaki sauce, drizzle with more sauce, and serve with boiled rice, sprinkled with the extra chopped scallion.

**For marinated miso chicken**, mix together 3 tablespoons miso paste, 2 tablespoons honey, and 4 tablespoons sake or dry sherry. Add the diced chicken and crushed garlic, omitting the ginger, and marinate in the refrigerator for at least 30 minutes. Thread alternately onto skewers with the scallions and peppers. Cook as above, brushing with the marinade from time to time.

# melanzane parmigiana

Serves **6**
Preparation time **40 minutes**
Cooking time **50 minutes,**
   **plus standing**

6 **eggplants**
2 tablespoons **olive oil**
2 cups grated **cheddar**
   **cheese**
½ cup grated **Parmesan**
   **cheese**
**salt**

**Tomato sauce**
2 tablespoons **olive oil**
1 large **onion,** chopped
2 **garlic cloves,** finely chopped
14 oz can **chopped tomatoes**
**salt** and **pepper**

**Make** the tomato sauce, by first heating the olive oil in a skillet. Fry the onion for 5 minutes, then add the garlic, add the tomatoes and cook, gently, for 10 minutes. Season well and keep warm.

**Trim** the ends off the eggplants and cut them lengthwise into thick slices. Sprinkle generously with salt and set aside for about 10 minutes. Wash well, drain, and pat dry on paper towels.

**Brush** the eggplant slices with oil, and place them on 2 large baking sheets. Roast the eggplants in a preheated oven, 400°F, for 10 minutes on each side until golden and tender. Do not turn off the oven.

**Spoon** a little of the tomato sauce into an ovenproof dish, and top with a layer of roasted eggplant and some of the cheddar. Continue with the layers, finishing with the cheddar. Sprinkle over the Parmesan, and bake for 30 minutes until bubbling and golden. Remove from the oven, and allow to stand for 5–10 minutes. Serve with a crisp green salad and crusty bread to mop up the juices.

**For eggplants with mozzarella & mint**, bake the eggplants and make the tomato sauce as above. Layer alternately in an ovenproof dish with 2 x 5 oz drained and sliced mozzarella cheeses and 2 tablespoons chopped mint. Sprinkle the top layer with ½ cup grated Parmesan cheese and bake as above.

# tuna & corn pilaf

Serves **4**
Preparation time **10 minutes**
Cooking time **15–20 minutes**

2 tablespoons **olive oil**
1 **onion**, chopped
1 **red bell pepper**, cored,
  seeded, and diced
1 **garlic clove**, crushed
1 ¼ cups **easy-cook
  long-grain rice**
3 cups **chicken stock**
11 oz can **corn kernels**,
  drained
7 oz can **tuna in spring water**,
  drained
**salt** and **pepper**
6 chopped **scallions**, to
  garnish

**Put** the oil in a saucepan over a low heat. Add the onion and red pepper and cook gently for about 5 minutes until softened. Add the garlic and cook for another 30 seconds. Stir in the rice, then pour over the stock and season with salt and pepper.

**Bring** to a boil, then reduce the heat and simmer, stirring occasionally, for 10–15 minutes until all the stock has been absorbed and the rice is tender.

**Stir** in the corn and tuna, and cook briefly over a low heat to heat through. Serve immediately garnished with the scallions.

**For picnic pilaf cake**, put the cooked rice mixture in a 9 inch square nonstick cake pan. In a bowl, whisk together 4 eggs and 4 tablespoons finely chopped flat-leaf parsley. Season well with salt and pepper and pour over the rice mixture. Bake in a preheated oven, 350°F, for 25–30 minutes until set. Allow to cool, then remove from the pan and serve cut into thick wedges.

# quick pasta carbonara

Serves **4**
Preparation time **10 minutes**
Cooking time **10 minutes**

13 oz **dried spaghetti** or other
   long, thin pasta
2 tablespoons **olive oil**
7 oz **pancetta**, cut into cubes
3 **eggs**
4 tablespoons freshly grated
   **Parmesan cheese**
3 tablespoons chopped **flat-
   leaf parsley**
3 tablespoons **light cream**
**salt** and **pepper**

**Cook** the pasta in a large saucepan of boiling salted water according to the package instructions until al dente.

**Meanwhile,** heat the oil in a large nonstick skillet over a medium heat. Add the pancetta and cook, stirring frequently, for 4–5 minutes until crisp.

**Whisk** together the eggs, Parmesan, parsley, and cream in a bowl. Season with salt and pepper and set aside.

**Drain** the pasta and add to the pancetta in the skillet. Stir over a low heat until combined, then pour in the egg mixture. Stir and remove the pan from the heat. Continue stirring for a few seconds until the eggs are lightly cooked and creamy. Serve immediately.

**For blue cheese & bacon carbonara**, cook the spaghetti as above. Fry 7 oz diced bacon in 2 tablespoons olive oil until golden. Add the drained pasta, 4 oz crumbled Stilton or Danish blue cheese, 3 tablespoons chopped flat-leaf parsley, and 3 tablespoons light cream. Season with a little salt and pepper. Cook and serve as above.

# leeks baked with blue cheese

Serves **4**
Preparation time **5 minutes**
Cooking time **30–35 minutes**

1½ lb **leeks**, trimmed, cleaned,
and cut into 3 and halved
lengthwise
2 tablespoons **hazelnut oil**
4 tablespoons **vegetable
stock**
1 tablespoon **butter**
4 oz **Dolcelatte cheese**,
crumbled
2 tablespoons toasted
**blanched hazelnuts**,
chopped
**salt** and **pepper**

**Toss** the leeks with the oil in a bowl, then put in
a shallow ovenproof dish with the stock. Bake in a
preheated oven, 400°F, for 15 minutes.

**Dot** the leeks with the butter, cheese, and nuts, then
return to the oven and cook for another 15–20 minutes
until the leeks are tender, the cheese has melted, and
the hazelnuts are golden. Sprinkle with salt and pepper
and serve immediately.

**For creamy leeks with Cheddar**, prepare the leeks
as above. Put in an ovenproof dish with 1 chopped
garlic clove and pour over 1¼ cups heavy cream.
Season with salt and pepper. Sprinkle with 2
tablespoons grated cheddar cheese and bake for
25–30 minutes, or until golden.

# salmon with horseradish crust

Serves **4**
Preparation time **10 minutes**
Cooking time **12–15 minutes**

4 **salmon fillets,** about 7 oz
   each, skin on and pin-boned
4 tablespoons **mild
   horseradish sauce**
2 cups **fresh bread crumbs**
20 **fresh asparagus spears,**
   trimmed
1 tablespoon **olive oil**
4–5 tablespoons **sour cream**
4 tablespoons **lemon juice**
1 tablespoon chopped **flat-
   leaf parsley**
**salt** and **pepper**

**Place** the salmon fillets in an ovenproof dish, skin side down. Spread the top of each fillet with 1 tablespoon of the horseradish sauce, then sprinkle with the bread crumbs. Roast in a preheated oven, 350°F, for 12–15 minutes until the fish is just cooked and the bread crumbs are golden brown.

**Meanwhile,** blanch the asparagus in salted boiling water for 2 minutes, then drain. Place in a very hot ridged griddle pan with the oil and grill for a couple of minutes on each side until slightly charred and just tender. Season with salt and pepper.

**Mix** together the sour cream, lemon juice, and parsley in a small bowl and season with salt and pepper.

**Serve** the salmon with the chargrilled asparagus and lemon sour cream.

**For roasted salmon with horseradish sauce**, season the salmon with salt and pepper and roast in the oven as above. Add 1 finely chopped shallot to a little olive oil in a pan and cook until softened. Remove from the heat and add 2 tablespoons horseradish sauce and 6 tablespoons sour cream. Season with salt and pepper. Serve with the roasted salmon.

# ginger beef with peppers

Serves **3–4**

Preparation time **10 minutes**, plus marinating

Cooking time **about 5 minutes**

1 lb lean **sirloin** or **tenderloin steak**, thinly sliced

2 teaspoons **light soy sauce**

2 tablespoons **sesame oil**

1 inch piece of **fresh ginger root**, peeled and sliced

2 teaspoons **rice vinegar**

1 tablespoon **water**

1 teaspoon **salt**

1 teaspoon **cornstarch**

1 **garlic clove**, crushed

pinch of **five-spice powder**

1 **red bell pepper**, cored, seeded, and cut into chunks

1 **green bell pepper**, cored, seeded, and cut into chunks

slivers of **fresh red chili**, to garnish (optional)

**Put** the slices of steak in a bowl and add the soy sauce, 1 teaspoon of the sesame oil, ginger, vinegar, measurement water, salt, and cornstarch. Stir well to mix and thoroughly coat the steak slices. Cover and let marinate in the refrigerator for at least 20 minutes.

**Heat** the remaining sesame oil in a wok or skillet over a high heat. Add the garlic and five-spice powder. Stir-fry for 30 seconds until the garlic is just opaque, then add the marinated steak; reserve any remaining marinade. Stir-fry the beef quickly for a couple of minutes until it is browned on the outside yet pink and tender on the inside, working in batches if necessary to avoid stewing the meat. Remove and set aside.

**Add** the red and green peppers to the wok or skillet and stir-fry briskly for 2–3 minutes, tossing them in the oil. Return the steak and the reserved marinade to the pan. Stir-fry for 1 minute until the meat is heated through. Transfer to a serving dish and garnish with thin slivers of chili, if desired. Serve immediately with straight-to-wok noodles or boiled rice.

**For gingered tofu with peppers**, thickly slice 1 lb well-drained chilled tofu and arrange on a foil-lined broiler rack. Mix 1 tablespoon sesame oil, 3 tablespoons light soy sauce, and a 1 inch piece of finely chopped ginger root in a bowl and spoon over the top of the tofu. Allow to marinate for 20 minutes, then broil for 4–5 minutes under a preheated hot broiler, turning once. Meanwhile, heat 1 tablespoon sesame oil in a wok, add the garlic, five-spice powder, and red and green peppers as above and stir-fry for 2–3 minutes. Add the tofu, toss through, and serve hot sprinkled with fresh chili, if desired.

# carrot, pea, & fava bean risotto

Serves **4**
Preparation time **15 minutes**
Cooking time **about 30 minutes**

6 cups **vegetable stock**
4 tablespoons **butter**
2 tablespoons **olive oil**
1 large **onion**, finely chopped
2 **carrots**, finely chopped
2 **garlic cloves**, finely chopped
1¾ cups **risotto rice**
¾ cup **white wine**
1⅓ cups **frozen peas**, thawed
⅔ cup **frozen fava beans**, thawed and peeled
½ cup finely grated **Parmesan cheese**
handful of **flat-leaf parsley**, roughly chopped
**salt** and **pepper**

**Pour** the stock into a saucepan and heat until just simmering. Keep hot.

**Melt** the butter with the oil in a saucepan over a low heat. Add the onion and carrots and cook gently for about 5 minutes until the onion is soft and translucent. Add the garlic and cook for another 1 minute until the garlic is opaque. Stir in the rice and continue stirring for a couple of minutes until the grains are coated with the butter mixture. Pour in the wine and cook rapidly, stirring, until the alcohol has evaporated.

**Add** the hot stock, a ladleful at a time, and cook over a low heat, stirring constantly, until each addition has been absorbed before adding the next. Continue until all the stock has been absorbed and the rice is creamy and cooked, but still retains a little bite—this will take around 15 minutes. (Be careful not to overcook.)

**Add** the peas and fava beans and heat through for 3–5 minutes. Remove from the heat and stir in the Parmesan and chopped parsley. Season with salt and pepper and serve immediately.

**For Italian-style risotto balls**, leave the risotto to cool, then chill overnight in the refrigerator. Form the chilled mixture into walnut-size balls. Whisk together 2 eggs in a shallow bowl. Roll the rice balls through the egg, then in 1 cup dried bread crumbs to coat. Fill a deep heavy saucepan one-third full with vegetable oil and heat to 350° to 375°F, or until a cube of bread browns in 30 seconds. Add the rice balls, in batches, and cook for 2–3 minutes until golden. Remove with a slotted spoon, drain on paper towels, and serve.

# shrimp laksa

Serves **1**
Preparation time **20 minutes**
Cooking time **15 minutes**

4 oz **rice noodles**
1 teaspoon **olive oil**
½ **red bell pepper**, cored, seeded, and sliced
1 cup **mushrooms**, sliced
1 teaspoon **laksa paste** or **Thai red** or **green curry paste**
⅔ cup **fish stock**
⅔ cup **coconut milk**
4 **raw jumbo shrimp**, peeled and deveined
2 **scallions**, sliced
1 tablespoon chopped **fresh cilantro**

**Put** the noodles in a bowl, cover with boiling water, and allow to soften for about 5 minutes or according to the package instructions (the time needed for soaking will depend on the thickness of the noodles you use). Drain in a colander, rinse under cold water, and set aside.

**Heat** the oil in a saucepan over a medium heat. Add the red pepper and mushrooms, and cook for 3–4 minutes until softened. Add the laksa or curry paste and cook, stirring, for 1 minute until fragrant.

**Pour** in the stock and coconut milk, and bring to a boil. Reduce the heat and simmer for 5 minutes.

**Add** the shrimp, scallions, drained noodles, and cilantro, stir to mix, and cook for 3–4 minutes until the shrimp have turned pink and are just cooked through. Serve immediately.

**For tuna & pea laksa**, prepare the noodles as above. Fry the mushrooms in the oil, omitting the pepper, then add the curry paste, followed by the stock, coconut milk, and ⅔ cup frozen peas. Simmer for 5 minutes, then mix in a 7 oz can drained tuna instead of the shrimp, adding the scallions, drained noodles, and cilantro. Simmer for 3–4 minutes until heated through.

# pork & rosemary pasta sauce

Serves **4**
Preparation time **20 minutes**
Cooking time **45 minutes**

3 tablespoons **olive oil**, plus
    extra, for drizzling
½ **onion**, finely chopped
1 **carrot**, finely diced
2 **celery sticks**, finely diced
2 **garlic cloves**, finely chopped
12 oz **pork tenderloin**, cut
    into ½ inch cubes
2 teaspoons finely chopped
    **rosemary**, plus few leaves to
    garnish (optional)
finely grated zest of ½ **lemon**
13 oz can **chopped tomatoes**
¾ cup **chicken stock**
**salt** and **pepper**
½ cup freshly grated
    **Parmesan cheese**, to serve

**Heat** the oil in a saucepan over a low heat and gently fry the onion for 5 minutes until soft and golden. Add the carrot, celery, and garlic and fry gently for another 5 minutes.

**Stir** in the pork, rosemary, and lemon zest, and fry for a few minutes until the pork is lightly browned all over. Season with salt and pepper.

**Add** the tomatoes and stock. Bring to a boil, then gently simmer over a low heat for 30 minutes. Serve hot with rigatoni or penne pasta, drizzled with a little extra olive oil and garnished with the rosemary, if desired. Serve the grated Parmesan in a bowl at the table for sprinkling over the top.

**For pork & basil gnocchi**, follow the recipe as above, frying the pork with the lemon zest and 2 tablespoons roughly torn basil leaves instead of the rosemary. Add the tomatoes and stock and continue cooking the meat sauce as above. Toss with 1 lb ready-made vacuum-packed gnocchi that has been cooked in a saucepan of boiling water according to the package instructions and drained well.

# lemon chicken with yogurt sauce

Serves **4**

Preparation time **10 minutes**, plus marinating

Cooking time **35–45 minutes**

4 **chicken quarters**

2 **lemons**, cut in half

1 tablespoon **dried oregano**

2 sprigs of **thyme**

4 tablespoons **olive oil**

4 **garlic cloves**, roughly chopped

**Yogurt sauce**

1 cup **whole milk yogurt**

1–2 **garlic cloves**

½ teaspoon **salt**

1 tablespoon chopped **dill weed**

**Rub** the chicken quarters all over, quite hard, with the cut lemons. Place the chicken quarters in a bowl or shallow dish. Add the oregano, thyme, olive oil, garlic, and rubbed lemon halves and mix everything together well. Cover with plastic wrap and allow to marinate in the refrigerator for at least 2 hours.

**Meanwhile,** make the yogurt sauce. Pour the yogurt into a bowl and beat until smooth. Mash together the garlic and salt in a bowl, then stir into the yogurt with the dill. Set aside.

**Transfer** the marinated chicken to a roasting pan and roast in a preheated oven, 400°F, for 35–45 minutes, spooning over a bit of the marinade now and then if the chicken looks too dry or burnt. To test whether the chicken is cooked through, pierce at the thickest point with a skewer—if the juices run clear, it is ready.

**Serve** with the yogurt sauce and a big plate of piping-hot French fries and salad leaves.

**For chicken salad with yogurt sauce**, cook the chicken as above, then let cool. Take the meat off the bones and cut into chunks. Mix into the yogurt sauce. Divide 2 cups of mixed salad leaves among 4 plates, then spoon the chicken salad on top. Alternatively, spoon into toasted and split pita breads, if desired.

# mango & shrimp curry

Serves **4**
Preparation time **10 minutes**
Cooking time **25 minutes**

3 **garlic cloves**, crushed
2 teaspoons finely grated
   **fresh ginger root**
2 tablespoons **ground cilantro**
2 teaspoons **ground cumin**
1 teaspoon **chili powder**
1 teaspoon **paprika**
½ teaspoon **ground turmeric**
1 tablespoon **grated jaggery**
   or **palm sugar** or **light
   brown sugar**
1²/₃ cups **water**
1 **green mango**, pitted and
   thinly sliced
1²/₃ cups **half-fat coconut
   milk**
1 tablespoon **tamarind paste**
1¼ lb **raw jumbo shrimp**,
   peeled and deveined
1 small bunch of **fresh cilantro**
**salt**

**Put** the garlic, ginger, ground cilantro, cumin, chili powder, paprika, turmeric, and jaggery or sugar in a large wok. Pour in the measurement water and stir to mix well. Place the wok over a high heat and bring the mixture to a boil. Reduce the heat and cook, covered, for 8–10 minutes.

**Add** the mango, coconut milk, and tamarind paste and stir to combine. Bring the mixture back to a boil, then add the shrimp.

**Stir** then reduce the heat, and simmer gently for 6–8 minutes. Tear some of the cilantro leaves into the curry (reserve the rest to use as a garnish) and cook for another 2 minutes until the shrimp have turned pink and are just cooked through. Season with a little salt and serve immediately with steamed basmati rice, garnished with the reserved sprigs of cilantro.

**For chicken & sweet potato curry**, simmer the spices in the measurement water as above. Omit the mango and shrimp and add 1 small peeled and diced sweet potato and 1 lb diced boneless, skinless chicken breasts with the coconut milk and 1 tablespoon tamarind paste. Bring to a boil, reduce the heat and simmer gently for 20 minutes until the chicken is cooked through. Add the cilantro and serve as above.

# lentil moussaka

Serves **4**
Preparation time **10 minutes**
Cooking time **45 minutes**,
  plus standing

½ cup **brown** or **green lentils**,
  picked over, rinsed and
  drained
13 oz can **chopped tomatoes**
2 **garlic cloves**, crushed
½ teaspoon **dried oregano**
pinch of **grated nutmeg**
²/₃ cup **vegetable stock**
2–3 tablespoons
  **vegetable oil**
8 oz **eggplant**, sliced
1 **onion**, finely chopped

**Cheese topping**
1 **egg**
²/₃ cup **cream cheese**
pinch of **grated nutmeg**
**salt** and **pepper**

**Put** the lentils in a saucepan with the tomatoes, garlic, oregano, and nutmeg. Pour in the stock. Bring to a boil, then reduce the heat and simmer for 20 minutes until the lentils are tender but not mushy, topping up with extra stock as needed.

**Meanwhile** heat the oil in a skillet and lightly fry the eggplant and onion, until the onion is soft and the eggplant is golden on both sides.

**Layer** the eggplant mixture and lentil mixture alternately in an ovenproof dish.

**Make** the topping. In a bowl, beat together the egg, cheese, and nutmeg with a good dash of salt and pepper. Pour over the moussaka and cook in a preheated oven, 400°F, for 20–25 minutes.

**Remove** from the oven and let stand for 5 minutes before serving with salad leaves.

**For moussaka baked potatoes**, cook 4 scrubbed baking potatoes in a preheated oven, 400°F, for about 1 hour until tender, or microwave if preferred. Meanwhile, make the lentil mixture as above. Fry the eggplant and onion separately, then stir into the lentils when cooked. Spoon over the slit potatoes, then top each one with a spoonful of cream cheese and a sprinkling of grated cheddar cheese.

# chicken thighs with fresh pesto

Serves **4**

Preparation time **5 minutes**

Cooking time **25 minutes**

1 tablespoon **olive oil**

8 **boneless, skinless chicken thighs**

**Pesto**

6 tablespoons **olive oil**

1/3 cup **pine nuts**, toasted

1/2 cup freshly grated **Parmesan cheese**

1 cup **basil leaves**, plus extra to garnish

1/2 cup roughly chopped **flat-leaf parsley**

2 **garlic cloves**, chopped

**salt** and **pepper**

**Heat** the oil in a nonstick skillet over a medium heat, add the chicken thighs, and pan-fry gently, turning frequently, for 20 minutes or until cooked through.

**Put** all the the pesto ingredients in a blender or food processor and blend until smooth.

**Remove** the chicken from the pan and set aside to keep warm. Reduce the heat to as low as possible, add the pesto, and heat through very gently for 2–3 minutes.

**Pour** the warmed pesto over the chicken thighs, garnish with extra basil, and serve with roasted Mediterranean vegetables (see below), steamed vegetables or a spinach salad.

**For roasted Mediterranean vegetables**, add 1 lb scrubbed baby new potatoes to a roasting pan, halving any large ones. Add 1/2 red bell pepper and 1/2 yellow bell pepper, both cored, seeded, and cut into chunks, 1 red onion, cut into chunks, 1 sliced large zucchini, and 2–3 roughly chopped garlic cloves. Drizzle with 3 tablespoons olive oil and roast in a preheated oven, 400°F, for 30 minutes, turning once, until the potatoes are golden.

# farfalle with tuna sauce

Serves **4**
Preparation time **10 minutes**,
  plus infusing
Cooking time **about 12
  minutes**

½ cup **canned tuna in
  olive oil**, drained
2 tablespoons **extra virgin
  olive oil**, plus extra, for
  drizzling (optional)
4 ripe **tomatoes**, roughly
  chopped
⅓ cup **pitted black olives**,
  roughly chopped
grated zest of **1 lemon**
2 **garlic cloves**, crushed
2 tablespoons roughly
  chopped **flat-leaf parsley**
12 oz **dried farfalle pasta**
**salt**

**Put** the drained tuna in a large serving bowl. Break it up
with a fork, then stir in the remaining ingredients except
for the pasta. Season with salt, cover, and allow to stand
for at least 30 minutes (including the pasta's cooking
time), to allow the flavors to infuse.

**Cook** the pasta in a large saucepan of salted boiling
water according to the package instructions until
al dente, then drain. Toss with the tuna mixture. Serve
immediately with a drizzle of extra virgin olive oil,
if desired.

### For farfalle with salami & basil sauce, mix
2 tablespoons olive oil with 2 teaspoons ready-
made pesto. Add 3 oz diced salami and 1 cup sliced
mushrooms and stir through. Next, add 4 chopped
tomatoes, the grated zest of 1 lemon, 2 crushed garlic
cloves, and 2 tablespoons roughly chopped fresh basil
or flat-leaf parsley. Toss with the cooked and drained
pasta as above.

# broiled pork steaks with sage

Serves **4**

Preparation time **5 minutes**,
plus marinating

Cooking time **10 minutes**

4 **pork steaks**, about
7 oz each

2 **garlic cloves**, finely chopped

1½ tablespoons finely
chopped **sage**

1 teaspoon **olive oil**

**salt** and **pepper**

**Cut** a horizontal pocket through the centre of each pork steak.

**Combine** the garlic, sage, and oil in a small bowl, then rub this mixture all over the outside and inside of the pork steaks. Place in a shallow dish, cover with plastic wrap, and allow to marinate in the refrigerator for at least 30 minutes or overnight.

**Season** the outside and inside of the pork steaks with salt and pepper, then place on a baking sheet lined with foil. Cook under a preheated very hot broiler, about 4 inches from the heat, for 5 minutes. Turn the pork steaks over and cook for another 5 minutes or until cooked through and golden. Serve with mashed sweet potato, or ordinary mashed potato if you prefer.

**For pork steaks with sage & cornmeal**, trim any excess fat from 8 thin-cut pork steaks, about 4 oz each. Mix 1½ cups instant cornmeal with ½ cup freshly grated Parmesan cheese and 1½ tablespoons chopped sage. Beat 2 eggs in a shallow dish, dip the pork steaks into the beaten egg, then coat in the cornmeal mixture. Pan-fry the steaks in 2–3 tablespoons olive oil for 15 minutes, turning until golden and cooked through. Serve with salad.

classic
favorites

# classic bolognese

Serves **4**
Preparation time **10 minutes**
Cooking time **4–6 hours**

2 tablespoons **unsalted butter**
1 tablespoon **olive oil**
1 small **onion**, finely chopped
2 **celery sticks**, finely chopped
1 **carrot**, finely chopped
1 **bay leaf**
7 oz **lean ground beef**
7 oz **lean ground pork**
²/₃ cup **dry white wine**
²/₃ cup **milk**
large pinch of freshly grated **nutmeg**
2 x 13 oz cans **chopped tomatoes**
1½–2½ cups **chicken stock**
13 oz dried or fresh **tagliatelle** or **fettuccine**
**salt** and **pepper**
freshly grated **Parmesan cheese**, to serve

**Melt** the butter with the oil in a large heavy saucepan over a low heat. Add the onion, celery, carrot, and bay leaf. Cook, stirring occasionally, for 10 minutes until softened but not browned. Add the meat, season with salt and pepper, and cook over a medium heat, stirring and breaking up the meat with a wooden spoon, until no longer pink.

**Pour** in the wine and bring to a boil. Gently simmer for 15 minutes until evaporated. Stir in the milk and nutmeg, and simmer for an additional 15 minutes until the milk has evaporated. Stir in the tomatoes and simmer very gently, uncovered, over a very low heat for 3–5 hours. The sauce is very thick, so when it begins to stick, add ½ cup of the stock at a time, as needed.

**Cook** the pasta in a large saucepan of salted boiling water until al dente: according to the package instructions for dried pasta or for 2 minutes if you are using fresh pasta. Drain thoroughly, reserving a ladleful of the cooking water.

**Return** the pasta to the pan and place over a low heat. Add the sauce and stir for 30 seconds, then pour in the reserved pasta cooking water and stir until the pasta is well coated and looks silky. Serve immediately with a sprinkling of grated Parmesan.

**For rich pork & chicken liver bolognese**, dice 4 oz chicken livers and 4 oz pancetta and cook with the onion and celery mixture as above. Omit the beef and use 7 oz ground pork and proceed as in the recipe above.

# chicken & mushroom pie

Serves **4**

Preparation time **20 minutes**

Cooking time **about 35 minutes**

2 tablespoons **vegetable oil**

1 **onion**, chopped

1 **garlic clove**, crushed

1 cup sliced **mushrooms**, sliced

1 tablespoon **all-purpose flour**

1¼ cups **chicken stock**

1 lb **cooked chicken**, cut into cubes

1 tablespoon chopped **flat-leaf parsley**

12 oz **ready-made puff pastry** (preferably made with butter), thawed if frozen

**beaten egg**, to glaze

**salt** and **pepper**

**Heat** the oil in a skillet over a medium heat. Add the onion and fry for about 5 minutes, stirring occasionally, until soft and translucent. Add the garlic and mushrooms and cook for another 2 minutes.

**Remove** the pan from the heat and stir in the flour. Slowly add the stock, a little at a time, and stir until well mixed. Return the pan to the heat and bring to a boil, stirring until thick and smooth.

**Stir** in the cooked chicken and parsley. Season with salt and pepper. Mix well, then put in a 5 cup pie dish or similar-sized ovenproof dish.

**Roll** out the pastry on a lightly floured surface to a shape just larger than the dish and put it over the pie. Brush the edge of the pie dish with beaten egg, add the pastry lid, press on to the dish edge then trim any excess pastry. Push down the edges to seal, crimping the edges with a finger and a small knife. Using a sharp knife, decorate the top of the pastry with crisscross lines, brush with the beaten egg, and bake in a preheated oven, 400°F, for 30 minutes until the pastry is puffed and golden brown.

**For chicken & mushroom potato pie**, peel and cut 1 lb floury potatoes and 8 oz rutabaga into chunks. Cook in a saucepan of boiling water for 15 minutes until tender. Drain, tip back into the pan, and mash with 2 tablespoons butter and 3 tablespoons milk. Season with salt and pepper. Spoon over the hot chicken and mushroom filling in the pie dish, dot with 2 tablespoons extra butter and cook under a preheated very hot broiler for a few minutes until golden. Serve hot.

# fish & chips

Serves **4**

Preparation time **25 minutes**

Cooking time **30 minutes**

1 cup **self-rising flour**, plus
   extra for dusting

½ teaspoon **baking powder**

¼ teaspoon **ground turmeric**

¾ cup **cold water**

3 lb large **round white** or
   **red potatoes**

1½ lb piece of **cod** or
   **haddock fillet**, skinned and
   pin-boned

**sunflower oil**, for deep-frying

**salt** and **pepper**

**Mix** together the flour, baking powder, turmeric, and a pinch of salt in a bowl and make a well in the center. Pour half the measurement water into it. Gradually whisk the flour into the water to make a smooth batter, then whisk in the remaining water. Set aside.

**Cut** the potatoes into ¾ inch slices, then cut across to make chunky fries. Put them in a bowl of cold water. Pat the fish dry on paper towels and cut into 4 portions. Season lightly with salt and pepper and dust with extra flour. Thoroughly drain the fries and pat them dry on paper towels. Pour the oil into a deep-fat fryer or deep, heavy saucepan to a depth of at least 3 inches and heat to 350°–375°F, or until a teaspoonful of batter turns golden in 30 seconds. Fry half the fries for 10 minutes or until golden. Drain and keep warm while you cook the remainder. Keep all the fries warm while you fry the fish.

**Dip** 2 pieces of fish in the batter, then carefully lower them into the hot oil. Fry gently for 4–5 minutes until crisp and golden. Drain and keep warm while you fry the rest. Serve with the fries.

**For tomato chutney**, to serve as an accompaniment, roughly chop 2½ lb tomatoes and finely chop 1 onion. Tip into a saucepan, including any juices from the tomatoes, with ⅔ cup superfine sugar and ⅔ cup malt vinegar. Bring to a boil, then reduce the heat and simmer gently for 1 hour or until sticky, stirring frequently. Pot the chutney into hot sterilized jars, cover with vinegar-proof lids, and seal tightly. Allow to cool, then store in a cool, dark place. Keep refrigerated once opened.

# spinach & potato omelet

Serves **4–6**

Preparation time **10 minutes**, plus cooling

Cooking time **about 45 minutes**

8 oz **waxy potatoes**, peeled and cut into ¾ inch dice
4 cups **baby spinach leaves**
2 tablespoons **olive oil**
1 small **onion**, finely chopped
6 large **eggs**
**salt** and **pepper**

**Cook** the potatoes in a saucepan of lightly salted boiling water until just tender; be careful not to overcook. Drain, then allow to cool.

**Rinse** the spinach and drain off the excess water in a colander. Put in a dry skillet over a medium heat with just the water clinging to the leaves from rinsing, cover, and cook for 2–3 minutes, shaking the pan from time to time, until just wilted. Squeeze out any remaining water, then roughly chop. Set aside.

**Heat** the oil in a 8 inch nonstick skillet with a flameproof handle (or cover the handle with foil) over a low heat. Add the onion and cook, stirring occasionally, for 8–10 minutes until softened. Add the cooled potatoes and cook, stirring, for 2–3 minutes. Add the reserved spinach and stir. Beat the eggs lightly in a bowl and season with salt and pepper. Pour into the pan over the vegetables and cook over a low heat, shaking frequently, for 10–12 minutes until set on the bottom.

**Put** the pan under a preheated medium broiler and cook for 2–3 minutes or until the top is set and lightly browned. Remove from the heat and allow to rest for 3–4 minutes before turning out onto a cutting board. Cut into wedges and serve with plain or chili ketchup.

**For bacon & pea omelet**, omit the spinach and fry 1 chopped onion with 4 diced bacon slices in the oil. Add the cooked diced potatoes as above, fry for 2–3 minutes, then add ½ cup frozen green peas. Cook for 2 minutes. Beat together the eggs and salt and pepper with 1 tablespoon chopped mint, if desired. Add to the pan and cook as above.

# shepherd's pie

Serves **4–6**

Preparation time **20 minutes**

Cooking time **about 1½ hours**

1 tablespoon **olive oil**

1 **onion**, finely chopped

1 **carrot**, diced

1 **celery stick**, diced

1 tablespoon chopped **thyme**

1 lb **ground lamb**

13 oz can **chopped tomatoes**

4 tablespoons **tomato paste**

1½ lb **round white** or **red potatoes**, peeled and cubed

¼ cup **butter**

3 tablespoons **milk**

¾ cup **cheddar cheese**, grated

**salt** and **pepper**

**Heat** the oil in a saucepan over a low heat. Add the onion, carrot, celery, and thyme, and cook gently for 10 minutes until soft and golden. Add the ground lamb and cook over a high heat, breaking up with a wooden spoon, for 5 minutes until browned. Add the tomatoes and tomato paste. Season with salt and pepper. Bring to a boil, then reduce the heat, cover, and simmer for 30 minutes. Remove the lid and cook for an additional 15 minutes to thicken.

**Put** the potatoes in a separate large saucepan of lightly salted water and bring to a boil. Reduce the heat and simmer for 15–20 minutes, while the lamb is cooking, until really tender. Drain the potatoes well and return to the pan. Mash in the butter, milk, and half the cheese, and season with salt and pepper.

**Spoon** the ground lamb mixture into an 8 cup ovenproof dish and carefully spoon the mash over the top, spreading over the surface of the filling. Run a fork through the top of the mash to fluff up slightly and sprinkle over the remaining cheese. Bake in a preheated oven, 375°F, for 20–25 minutes until bubbling and golden.

**For curried lamb phyllo pies**, prepare and cook the ground meat mixture as above, adding 1 tablespoon medium curry paste with the tomatoes and tomato paste. Spoon the filling into 1¼ cups ovenproof dishes. Omit the potato topping and instead layer 4 sheets of phyllo pastry together, brushing each one with a little melted butter. Cut into 6 and scrunch each over a dish to cover. Bake in a preheated oven, 375°F, for 20 minutes until the pastry is lightly golden.

# creamy pork & cider hotpot

Serves **4**

Preparation time **25 minutes**

Cooking time **1½ hours**

2 teaspoons **all-purpose flour**

1¼ lb **lean boneless leg of pork**, trimmed of any excess fat and cut into bite-size chunks

2 tablespoons **butter**

1 tablespoon **olive oil**

1 small **onion**, chopped

1 large **leek**, trimmed, cleaned, and chopped

1¾ cups **cider**

1 tablespoon chopped **sage**

2 tablespoons **whole grain mustard**

2 **pears**

6 tablespoons **sour cream**

1 lb **sweet potatoes**, scrubbed and thinly sliced

2 tablespoons **chili oil**

**salt**

chopped **flat-leaf parsley**, to garnish

**Season** the flour with a little salt and use to coat the pieces of meat.

**Melt** the butter with the oil in a shallow flameproof casserole and gently fry the pork in batches until lightly browned. Remove each batch with a slotted spoon and set aside on a warm plate.

**Add** the onion and leek to the casserole, and fry gently for 5 minutes until soft and translucent. Return the meat to the pan, along with the cider, sage, and mustard. Bring just to a boil, then cover, reduce the heat to as low as possible, and simmer gently for 30 minutes.

**Peel**, core, and thickly slice the pears. Stir the sour cream into the sauce, then lay the pear slices on top. Arrange the sweet potato slices in overlapping layers on top, putting the end pieces underneath and keeping the best slices for the top layer. Brush with the chili oil and sprinkle with salt.

**Cook** in a preheated oven, 325°F, for 45 minutes or until the potatoes are tender and lightly browned. Sprinkle with the chopped parsley and serve hot.

**For creamy pork & white wine hotpot**, replace the cider with 1¾ cups dry white wine in the third step. Use 1 lb waxy potatoes instead of the sweet potatoes, and layer on top as above. Brush with the chili oil and sprinkle with salt, then cook in the oven for about 1 hour.

# fast chicken curry

Serves **4**
Preparation time **5 minutes**
Cooking time **20–25 minutes**

3 tablespoons **olive oil**
1 **onion**, finely chopped
4 tablespoons **medium curry paste**
8 **boneless, skinless chicken thighs**, cut into thin strips
13 oz can **chopped tomatoes**
8 oz **broccoli**, broken into small florets, stalks peeled and sliced
6 tablespoons **coconut milk**
**salt** and **pepper**

**Heat** the oil in a deep nonstick saucepan over a medium heat. Add the onion and cook for 3 minutes until soft and translucent. Add the curry paste and cook, stirring, for 1 minute until fragrant.

**Add** the chicken, tomatoes, broccoli, and coconut milk to the pan. Bring to a boil, then reduce the heat, cover and simmer gently over a low heat for 15–20 minutes until the chicken is cooked through.

**Remove** from the heat, season well with salt and pepper, and serve immediately.

**For seafood patties with curry sauce**, follow the first stage of the recipe above, then add the tomatoes, 4 cups young spinach leaves, and the coconut milk (omitting the chicken and broccoli), and cook as directed. Meanwhile, put 12 oz roughly chopped white fish fillets and 6 oz frozen cooked peeled and deveined shrimp, thawed and roughly chopped, in a food processor and process until well combined. Alternatively, finely chop and mix together by hand. Transfer to a bowl and add 4 finely chopped scallions, 2 tablespoons chopped fresh cilantro leaves, 1 cup fresh white bread crumbs, a squeeze of lemon juice, and 1 beaten egg. Season with salt and pepper. Mix well, then form into 16 patties. Roll in ½ cup fresh white bread crumbs to coat. Heat a shallow depth of vegetable oil in a large skillet over a medium heat. Add the patties, cooking in batches, and pan-fry for 5 minutes on each side or until crisp and golden brown an dooked through. Serve hot with the curry sauce.

# quick beef stroganoff

Serves **4**
Preparation time **10 minutes**
Cooking time **15 minutes**

2 tablespoons **paprika**
1 tablespoon **all-purpose flour**
1 lb **beef sirloin**, sliced
1½ cups **long-grain white rice**
2 tablespoons **butter**
4 tablespoons **vegetable or sunflower oil**
1 large **onion**, thinly sliced
8 oz **chestnut mushrooms**, trimmed and sliced
1¼ cups **sour cream**
**salt** and **pepper**
1 tablespoon chopped **curly parsley**, to garnish

**Mix** together the paprika and flour in a large bowl. Add the beef and turn to coat.

**Cook** the rice in lightly salted boiling water for 13 minutes or according to the package instructions until cooked but firm. Drain, set aside, and keep warm.

**Meanwhile,** melt the butter with 2 tablespoons of the oil in a large skillet over a low heat. Add the onion and cook for about 6 minutes until soft and translucent. Add the mushrooms and cook for another 5 minutes until soft. Remove with a slotted spoon and set aside.

**Add** the remaining oil to the pan, increase the heat to high, and add the beef. Fry until browned all over, working in batches if necessary, then reduce the heat. Return the onion mixture to the pan along with the sour cream. Stir through, bring to a boil, then reduce the heat and allow to bubble gently for 1–2 minutes. Season well with salt and pepper.

**Serve** immediately with the cooked rice and a sprinkling of chopped parsley.

**For mushroom & red pepper stroganoff**, omit the beef, increase the quantity of chestnut mushrooms to 1 lb and add 2 thinly sliced cored and seeded red bell peppers. Cook the mushrooms with the onion, stirring from time to time, until they have reduced and the onion is soft and translucent. Remove the mixture from the pan with a slotted spoon. Cook the peppers in the same pan until tender, then return the onion mixture to the pan and continue as above. Sprinkle with toasted pine nuts instead of the parsley, and serve on a bed of rice.

# fish pie

Serves **4**
Preparation time **15 minutes**
Cooking time **1 hour 10
minutes**

10 oz peeled and deveined
   **raw shrimp**, (thawed if
   frozen)
2 teaspoons **cornstarch**
10 oz **white fish fillets** such
   as haddock, skinned and cut
   into small pieces
2 teaspoons **green
   peppercorns in brine**,
   rinsed and drained
1 small **fennel bulb**,
   roughly chopped
1 small **leek**, trimmed, cleaned,
   and roughly chopped
1 ½ cups **dill weed**
¼ cup **flat-leaf parsley**
⅔ cup **fresh** or **frozen green
   peas**
1 ½ cups **ready-made cheese
   sauce**
1 ½ lb **baking potatoes**,
   thinly sliced
¾ cup grated **cheddar
   cheese**
**salt** and **pepper**

**Dry** the shrimp, if frozen and thawed, by patting
between sheets of paper towels. Season the cornstarch
with salt and pepper and use to coat the shrimp and
white fish. Lightly crush the peppercorns using a mortar
and pestle.

**Put** the peppercorns in a food processor with the
fennel, leek, dill, parsley, and a little salt and blend until
very finely chopped, scraping the mixture down from
the sides of the bowl if necessary. Tip into a shallow
ovenproof dish.

**Arrange** the shrimp and fish over the fennel mixture,
and mix together a little. Scatter the peas on top.

**Spoon** half the cheese sauce over the filling, and
spread roughly with the back of a spoon. Layer the
potatoes on top, overlapping the slices and seasoning
each layer with salt and pepper as you go. Spoon the
remaining sauce over the top, spreading it in a thin layer.
Sprinkle with the cheese.

**Bake** in a preheated oven, 425°F, for 30 minutes until
the surface has turned pale golden. Reduce the oven
temperature to 350°F and cook for an additional 30–40
minutes until the potatoes are completely tender and
the fish is cooked through. Serve with a tomato salad.

**For smoked fish & caper pie**, use 1 ¼ lb smoked
pollack fillets, skinned and cut into small chunks,
instead of the shrimp and white fish. Replace the green
peppercorns with 2 tablespoons rinsed and drained
salted capers and follow the recipe as above.

# chili con carne

Serves **4**
Preparation time **5 minutes**
Cooking time **about 1 hour**

2 tablespoons **vegetable oil**
2 **onions**, chopped
1 **red bell pepper**, cored,
   seeded, and cut into cubes
2 **garlic cloves**, crushed
1 lb **ground beef**
1¾ cups **beef stock**
½–1 teaspoon **chili powder**
1¾ cups **canned red kidney
   beans**, drained
13 oz can **chopped tomatoes**
1 tablespoon **tomato paste**
1 teaspoon **ground cumin**
**salt** and **pepper**
1¼ cups **long-grain
   white rice**

**To serve**
**sour cream**
**dried red pepper flakes**
**cheddar cheese**, grated
finely chopped **scallion**

**Heat** the oil in a saucepan over a low heat. Add the onions and red pepper and gently fry, stirring now and then, for about 5 minutes until soft. Add the garlic and cook for another 1 minute until opaque.

**Increase** the heat slightly and add the meat. Fry until just brown, stirring and breaking up the meat with a wooden spoon. Pour in the stock, then add the chili powder, beans, tomatoes, cumin, and a dash of salt and pepper.

**Bring** to a boil, then cover, reduce the heat to as low as possible and simmer very gently for 50–60 minutes, stirring occasionally so that it does not stick to the bottom of the pan.

**Cook** the rice, toward the end of the chili's cooking time, in lightly salted water, according to the package instructions, then drain.

**Pile** up the rice on each of 4 warm serving plates, dollop on the cooked chili and top with the sour cream. Sprinkle with the chili flakes, grated cheddar and scallions and serve immediately with the boiled rice.

**For veggie con carne**, heat the oil in a pan, add the onion, red pepper, and garlic as above, plus 1 diced eggplant. Fry, stirring, until softened, then add 2 diced zucchini and fry for a few minutes more, omitting the ground beef. Add the stock and remaining ingredients, and cook as above.

# chicken kiev

Serves **4**

Preparation time **40 minutes**,
   plus freezing and chilling

Cooking time **20 minutes**

½ cup **butter**, at room
   temperature

2 tablespoons chopped
   **chives**

1 tablespoon chopped **flat-
   leaf parsley**

2 teaspoons chopped
   **tarragon** (optional)

1 **garlic clove**, finely chopped

2 teaspoons **lemon juice**

4 **boneless, skinless chicken
   breasts**, about 15 oz each

2 tablespoons **all-purpose
   flour**

2½ cups **fresh white
   bread crumbs**

2 **eggs**

3 tablespoons **sunflower oil**

**pepper**

**Beat** the butter with the herbs, garlic, lemon juice, and
a little pepper in a small bowl. Spoon into a line about
10 inches long on a sheet of plastic wrap or foil, then
roll up into a neat log shape. Freeze for 15 minutes.

**Meanwhile**, put one of the chicken breasts between
two large sheets of plastic wrap and beat with a meat
mallet or the side of a rolling pin until the chicken forms
a rectangle about ⅛ inch thick, being careful not to
make any holes. Repeat with the other chicken breasts.
Cut the herb butter log into 4 pieces and put 1 piece
on each chicken breast. Fold in the sides of each one,
then the top and bottom, to make 4 tight parcels.

**Put** the flour on a plate and the bread crumbs on a
second plate then beat the eggs in a shallow dish.
Carefully roll the chicken parcels in the flour, then coat
in the egg and roll in the bread crumbs. Put the coated
parcels back onto the empty flour plate and chill for
1 hour (longer if you have time).

**Heat** the oil in a large skillet over a medium heat.
Add the chicken Kievs and fry for 5 minutes, turning
until evenly browned. Transfer to a baking sheet, then
complete cooking in a preheated oven, 400°F, for 15
minutes or until the chicken is cooked through. Serve
with braised red cabbage.

**For chicken, garlic, & sundried tomato Kievs**, chop
1 cup drained sundried tomatoes in oil and stir into
⅔ cup garlic and herb cream cheese. Divide between the
flattened chicken breasts, then shape, chill, and cook as
above.

# vegetable lasagna

Serves **4**
Preparation time **10 minutes**
Cooking time **1¼ hours**,
    plus standing

2 tablespoons **vegetable oil**
1 cup chopped **French beans**
1 **onion**, thinly sliced
13 oz can **chopped tomatoes**
½ cup **split red lentils**, picked
    over, rinsed, and drained
1¼ cups **water**
pinch of **dried oregano**
2 cups **cream cheese**
2 **eggs**, beaten
4 oz **no-boil lasagna sheets**
2 tablespoons freshly grated
    **Parmesan cheese**
**salt** and **pepper**

**Heat** the oil in a saucepan over a low heat and fry the beans and onion for 5 minutes until the onion is soft and translucent.

**Sprinkle** with salt and pepper, then add the tomatoes, lentils, measurement water, and oregano. Bring to a boil. Simmer for about 30 minutes or until the lentils are tender but not mushy. Mix together the cream cheese and beaten eggs in a bowl.

**Spread** half the vegetable and lentil mixture over the bottom of a large ovenproof dish, then cover with a third of the lasagna sheets. Pour over half the cheese mixture, then cover with another layer of lasagna sheets. Make a layer with the remaining vegetable and lentil mixture, cover with the remaining lasagna sheets, and, finally, with the rest of the cheese mixture.

**Sprinkle** with the Parmesan and bake in a preheated oven, 350°F, for 40 minutes. Remove from the oven and allow to stand for 5 minutes before cutting into slices and serving.

**For beef lasagna**, fry the sliced onion in the oil for 5 minutes until soft, omitting the green beans. Increase the heat slightly and add 1 lb ground beef. Cook, stirring and breaking up the meat with a wooden spoon, until the meat is browned. Stir in 2 chopped garlic cloves, ½ teaspoon dried oregano, and 1 tablespoon all-purpose flour, then mix in the chopped tomatoes and ¾ cup beef stock. Simmer gently for 45 minutes, stirring now and then, until the meat is tender. Layer in an ovenproof dish with the lasagna and cream cheese mixture and cook as above.

# simple vegetable biriyani

Serves **4**
Preparation time **25 minutes**
Cooking time **about 1 hour**,
  plus standing

1¼ cups **basmati rice**
6 tablespoons **vegetable oil**
2 large **onions**, sliced
2 teaspoons grated peeled
  **fresh ginger root**
2 **garlic cloves**, crushed
8 oz **sweet potatoes**, peeled
  and cut into cubes
2 large **carrots**, cut into cubes
1 tablespoon **curry paste**
2 teaspoons **ground turmeric**
1 teaspoon **ground cinnamon**
1 teaspoon **chili powder**
1¼ cups **vegetable stock**
4 **tomatoes**, skinned, seeded,
  and cubed
½ cup **cauliflower florets**
¾ cup **frozen green peas**,
  thawed (optional)
⅓ cup **cashew nuts**
2 **hard-cooked eggs**, peeled
  and cut into quarters
**salt** and **pepper**

**Cook** the rice in a saucepan of boiling water for
5 minutes. Drain in a colander, run under cold water,
then drain again. Spread out the rice on a plate so
that it dries out a little.

**Heat** 2 tablespoons of the oil in a skillet over a medium
heat. Add half the onion and fry for 10 minutes until
very crisp and golden. Remove and set aside to drain
on paper towels. Add the rest of the oil to the skillet,
and fry the rest of the onion and ginger for 5 minutes
until the onion is soft and translucent, adding the garlic
for the last minute of the cooking time. Add the sweet
potatoes, carrots, curry paste, and spices and fry for
another 10 minutes until light golden.

**Pour** in the stock and add the tomatoes. Bring to a boil,
reduce the heat, cover, and simmer for 20 minutes. Add
the cauliflower and peas, if desired, and cook for 8–10
minutes until the vegetables are tender. Check the
seasoning and add salt and pepper if needed.

**Mix** in the rice and cashew nuts. Cook, stirring, for
3 minutes, then cover and remove from the heat. Allow to
stand for 5 minutes, then serve sprinkled with the crispy-
fried onions and topped with the hard-cooked eggs.

**For chicken biryani**, cook the rice and fry the onions for
topping as above. Fry 1 lb diced boneless, skinless chicken
breasts in the remaining oil with the diced carrots, curry
paste, and spices for 10 minutes, stirring until golden. Add
the stock and tomatoes and cook as above, adding ¾ cup
frozen green peas instead of the cauliflower. Cook for
5 minutes. Stir in the rice and cashew nuts. Serve with
the crispy-fried onion and egg as above.

# roast lamb with wine & juniper

Serves **6**

Preparation time **20 minutes**

Cooking time **1 hour 35 minutes**

2 tablespoons **olive oil**

1 **leg of lamb**, about 3 lb, trimmed of excess fat

10 **juniper berries**, crushed

3 **garlic cloves**, crushed

2 oz **salted anchovies**, boned and rinsed

1 tablespoon **chopped rosemary**

2 tablespoons **balsamic vinegar**

2 sprigs of **rosemary**

1¼ cups **dry white wine**

**salt** and **pepper**

**Heat** the oil in a roasting pan in which the lamb will fit snugly over a medium-high heat. Add the lamb and cook until browned all over. Allow to cool.

**Pound** 6 of the juniper berries, the garlic, anchovies and chopped rosemary with the end of a rolling pin in a bowl, or use a mortar and pestle. Stir in the vinegar and mix to a paste.

**Make** small incisions all over the lamb with a small, sharp knife. Spread the paste over the lamb, working it into the incisions. Season with salt and pepper. Put the rosemary sprigs in the roasting pan and sit the lamb on top. Pour in the white wine and add the remaining white juniper berries.

**Cover** the roasting pan with foil and bring to the boil on the stovetop, then cook in a preheated oven, 325°F, for 1 hour, turning the lamb every 20 minutes. Raise the temperature to 400°F, remove the foil, and roast for 30 minutes more until the lamb is very tender. Serve with roasted potatoes and steamed vegetables.

**For leg of lamb with lemon & rosemary**, omit the juniper berries and pound the grated zest of 2 lemons with the garlic, anchovies, and chopped rosemary. Replace the vinegar with 4 tablespoons lemon juice. Spoon the paste over the lamb, working it into the incisions as above, and continue with the rest of the recipe.

# traditional roast turkey

Serves **8**

Preparation time **45 minutes**, plus resting

Cooking time **3 hours 40 minutes**

10 lb **turkey**, giblets removed and cavity rinsed

1 package **ready-made stuffing**

1 tablespoon **dried basil**

**paprika**, for sprinkling

¼ cup **butter**

6 **bacon slices** (optional)

1 **lemon**, sliced

1 **orange**, sliced

**salt** and **pepper**

**Gravy**

2½ cups **chicken** or **vegetable stock**

6 tablespoons **port** or **white wine**

1 tablespoon **cornstarch**

**If** using a frozen bird, make sure that the turkey is completely thawed before using. Take the turkey out of the refrigerator a couple of hours before you intend to start cooking, to allow it to come to room temperature.

**Put** the turkey in a large roasting pan, make up the stuffing as packet instructions and use to stuff the neck of the bird. Sprinkle the turkey with the basil and paprika and season. Lay the bacon slices over the breast, if using, and tuck the lemon and orange slices around it. Loosely cover with foil, tucking the edges in around the edge of the roasting pan. Roast in a preheated oven, 350°F, for 20 minutes per 1 lb plus 20 minutes. Baste regularly.

**Remove** the foil 20 minutes before the end so that the turkey browns. Transfer the turkey to a warm serving dish, cover with foil, and let rest while you make the gravy. Skim off and discard the fat from the pan juices, then pour in the stock and port or wine, and bring to a boil. Stir in the cornstarch and some cold water to thicken the gravy. Carve the turkey and eat with roasted potatoes, carrots, and vegetables of your choice.

**For crispy roasted potatoes**, to accompany the turkey, peel and cut 3 lb potatoes into chunky pieces. Add to a saucepan of salted boiling water and cook for 8–10 minutes until the edges are just breaking up. Drain well, return to the pan, and shake. Heat 5 tablespoons sunflower oil or goose fat in a roasting tin on the shelf above the turkey for 2–3 minutes until very hot. Carefully add the potatoes to the pan, spooning the oil or fat on top. Roast in the oven for 1 hour, turning once or twice, until golden. Drain off the oil or fat and serve with the turkey.

# comfort food & snacks

# garlic bread

Serves **2**
Preparation time **5 minutes**
Cooking time **4 minutes**

4 slices of **bread** such as
   ciabatta, sourdough, French
   bread, or pita
2–3 **garlic cloves**, peeled
   and halved
½ cup **olive oil**
a little chopped **flat-leaf
   parsley** (optional)
**salt**

**Toast** the bread on both sides under a preheated
medium broiler until golden. While the bread is still
warm, rub one side with the cut sides of the garlic.

**Put** the warm toasted bread on a plate and drizzle
2 tablespoons of the olive oil over each slice. Sprinkle
with salt and a little chopped parsley, if desired, and
serve as a starter, snack, or with any pasta dish or salad.

**For tomato & basil bread**, toast the bread as
above and rub with the garlic, then mix the oil with
2 teaspoons sundried tomato paste (from a tube)
and 2 tablespoons chopped basil. Drizzle over the
toasted bread, then serve.

# poached eggs, bacon, & muffins

Serves **4**
Preparation time **5 minutes**
Cooking time **about
 20 minutes**

4 ripe **tomatoes**, thickly sliced
2 tablespoons chopped **basil**
2 tablespoons **olive oil**
8 **bacon slices**
4 split and toasted **English
 muffins**, buttered, or 4
 slices toasted **bread** such as
 ciabatta, buttered, to serve
4 large **eggs**
1 tablespoon **vinegar**
**salt** and **pepper**

**Lay** the tomato slices in a broiler pan. Mix together the basil and oil in a bowl, then drizzle over the tomatoes. Season with lots of salt and pepper. Cook under a preheated medium broiler for 3–4 minutes until starting to soften. Arrange the bacon slices on top of the tomatoes and grill for 6–8 minutes, turning once.

**Poach** the eggs, by breaking 1 of the eggs into a ramekin or cup, making sure not to break the yolk. Bring a large saucepan of water to a boil. Add the vinegar to the boiling water, then stir the water rapidly in a circular motion to make a whirlpool. Carefully slide the egg into the center of the pan while the water is still swirling, holding the ramekin or cup as close to the water as you can. Repeat with the other eggs and cook for 3 minutes. Lift the poached eggs out with a slotted spoon.

**Put** a hot buttered muffin or slice of toasted bread on a warm plate. Top half of the muffin or the toast with broiled tomatoes and 2 slices of bacon, then put the poached egg on top. Cook and serve the other 3 eggs in the same way, swirling the boiling water into a whirlpool each time before sliding in the egg. (Poaching the eggs separately ensures each serving is as fresh and hot as possible at the table.) Serve.

**For poached eggs with mushrooms**, omit the tomatoes, herbs, and bacon. Heat 2 tablespoons olive oil in a skillet, add 7 oz trimmed, sliced closed-cup white or chestnut mushrooms. Sauté, stirring, for a few minutes until softened and golden. Add 1 tablespoon Worcestershire sauce and 1 tablespoon ketchup and stir through. Spoon over toasted and buttered muffins and top each with a poached egg.

# baked tortillas with hummus

Serves **4**
Preparation time **5 minutes**
Cooking time **10–12 minutes**

4 small **soft flour tortillas**
1 tablespoon **olive oil**

**Hummus**

13 oz can **chickpeas**, drained
and rinsed
1 **garlic clove**, chopped
4 tablespoons **whole milk
yogurt**
2 tablespoons **lemon juice**
2 **garlic cloves**, peeled and
finely chopped
1 small bunch **fresh
cilantro**, chopped
**salt** and **pepper**
**paprika**, for sprinkling

**Make** the hummus first. Put the chickpeas in a bowl, and mash with a fork to break them up. Add the garlic, yogurt, lemon juice, and cilantro and season with salt and pepper. Mix together. Alternatively, put all the ingredients except the cilantro in a blender or food processor and blend to a coarse puree. Add the cilantro and whiz briefly until mixed through. Put the hummus in a serving bowl or dish and sprinkle with a little paprika.

**Cut** each tortilla into 8 triangles, put on a baking sheet, and brush with a little oil. Bake in a preheated oven, 400°F, for 10–12 minutes until golden and crisp. Remove from the oven.

**Serve** the tortilla triangles with the hummus for dipping or spreading on top.

**For baked tortillas with fava bean hummus**, cook 2½ cups frozen fava beans in boiling water for 4–5 minutes until tender. Drain, then mash or puree with the garlic, yogurt, lemon juice, salt, and pepper as above. Mix in 3 tablespoons chopped mint leaves, 1 chopped seeded fresh green chili, and 1 teaspoon ground cumin instead of the fresh cilantro.

# macaroni & haddock cheese

Serves **4**
Preparation time **2 minutes**
Cooking time **30 minutes**

2½ cups **milk**
11 oz **undyed smoked haddock fillets**
11 oz **dried macaroni**
¼ cup **unsalted butter**
¼ cup **all-purpose flour**
1 tablespoon **whole grain mustard**
1 cup **light cream**
²/₃ cup **shelled green peas**, thawed if frozen
1 cup **cheddar cheese**, grated
4 tablespoons freshly grated **Parmesan cheese**
1 tablespoon roughly chopped **flat-leaf parsley**
2 cups **fresh white** or **whole-wheat bread crumbs**
1 tablespoon **olive oil**
**salt** and **pepper**

**Heat** the milk to scalding point (just before boiling point) in a wide-based shallow saucepan. Add the haddock, in a single layer, and poach gently for 6–8 minutes until the flesh flakes easily. Lift the fish from the pan with a slotted spoon. Once the fish is cool enough to handle, remove and discard the skin and break the flesh into large flakes. Strain the milk in which the fish was cooked into a pitcher and set aside.

**Cook** the pasta in a large saucepan of salted boiling water until al dente. Meanwhile, melt the butter in a saucepan over a very low heat. Sprinkle in the flour and cook, stirring with a wooden spoon, for 2 minutes until the mixture is a light straw color. Remove the pan from the heat and slowly add the reserved milk, stirring away lumps. Return the pan to the heat and simmer, stirring, for 2–3 minutes until thickened and creamy. Stir in the mustard, cream, peas, cheddar, and half the Parmesan. Season with salt and pepper.

**Drain** the pasta and return to the pan. Fold the cheese sauce and haddock flakes into the pasta, then transfer to a greased ovenproof dish. Mix the parsley and remaining Parmesan into the bread crumbs, then sprinkle evenly over the pasta. Drizzle with the oil and bake in a preheated oven, 425°F, for 10 minutes until bubbling and golden.

**For tarragon carrots**, to serve as a side dish, blanch 8–10 oz halved baby carrots in boiling water for 2 minutes. Drain and return to the pan. Cook gently, with the lid on, in 2 tablespoons butter, 1 tablespoon olive oil, and 1 teaspoon sugar for 5 minutes until tender. Add 2 tablespoons chopped tarragon before serving.

# sausages with mustard mash

Serves **4**
Preparation time **5 minutes**
Cooking time **25 minutes**

8 good-quality **thick pork** or
    **beef sausages**
2 **onions**, cut into wedges

**Mustard mash**
2 lb **round white** or **red**
    **potatoes**, scrubbed and
    quartered (leave unpeeled)
$^1/_3$ cup **butter**
1–2 tablespoons **smooth**
    **Dijon mustard**
1 **garlic clove**, crushed
1 large bunch of **flat-leaf**
    **parsley**, chopped
dash of **olive oil**
**salt** and **pepper**

**Start** the mustard mash first. Put the potatoes in a
large saucepan of cold water, bring to a boil, and simmer
for 15 minutes until tender.

**Cook** the sausages, meanwhile, in a skillet over
a medium heat or under a preheated medium broiler
for 10 minutes, turning to get an even color. Add
the onion wedges and cook with the sausages for
6–7 minutes until softened and starting to brown.

**Drain** the potatoes well when they are cooked. Once
they are cool enough to handle, peel them and return
to the pan. Mash well, so that they are nice and creamy.

**Add** the butter, mustard, garlic, and a good sprinkling
of salt and pepper, and carry on mashing. Taste and
add more mustard, if desired. Finally, stir in the parsley
and a dash of olive oil.

**Pile** up a serving of the mash on each of 4 warm
plates and stick the sausages and onion wedges
on top. Serve immediately with gravy for pouring
over (see below).

**For caramelized onion gravy**, to accompany the
sausages, heat 1 tablespoon sunflower oil in a skillet
over low heat, add 1 large thinly sliced onion, and
fry gently for 10 minutes until just starting to brown.
Sprinkle with 1 teaspoon superfine sugar and cook for
5 minutes more, stirring until caramelized and browned.
Stir in 1 tablespoon all-purpose flour and cook for a
minute or so. Pour in 1 cup beef stock and season with
salt and pepper. Stir through. Simmer for 5 minutes,
stirring frequently. Serve hot.

# falafel burgers

Serves **4**

Preparation time **15 minutes**, **plus chiling**

Cooking time **8 minutes**

14 oz can **chickpeas**, drained and rinsed

2 **garlic cloves**, crushed

1 **small red onion**, finely chopped

2 teaspoons **ground cumin**

2 tablespoons each chopped **fresh cilantro** and **flat leaf parsley**

grated zest of 1 **lemon**

1 **egg yolk**

2 tablespoons **gram (besan)** or **all-purpose flour**

**vegetable oil** for frying

**salt** and **pepper**

**Garlic and mint sauce**

¾ cup **plain** or **whole milk yogurt**

2 tablespoons **chopped mint**

1 **garlic clove**, crushed

**To serve**

8 mini **pita breads**

6 tablespoons ready-made **red pepper** or ordinary **hummus**

**Put** all the ingredients for the falafel, except the flour and oil, in the bowl of a food processor. Season with salt and pepper, then process into a rough paste. Using slightly wet hands, divide the mixture into 8 equal-sized balls, flattening them a little to make burgers. Cover and chill for 30 minutes.

**Mix** together the yogurt, mint, and garlic in a small bowl. Season with salt and pepper, and set aside until needed.

**Coat** the chilled falafel burgers lightly with the gram or all-purpose flour. Pour just enough oil for pan-frying into a heavy skillet over a medium-high heat. When the oil is hot, carefully add the falafel burgers and fry for 4 minutes on each side until golden brown and crisp.

**Toast** the pita breads under a preheated hot broiler until warmed through but still soft. Spread each one with some hummus and top with the salad and a burger. Sprinkle with a little paprika, and serve immediately with the garlic mint sauce for spooning over the top.

# southern fried chicken

Serves **4**

Preparation time **25 minutes**

Cooking time **40–45 minutes**

6 tablespoons **sunflower oil**

1½ teaspoons **smoked paprika**

1½ teaspoons **dried oregano**

1 teaspoon **powdered mustard**

1 teaspoon **dried red pepper flakes**

1 lb **sweet potatoes**, peeled and cut into thick wedges

1 lb **round white** or **red potatoes**, scrubbed and cut into thick wedges

4 tablespoons **all-purpose flour**

2 **eggs**

2 tablespoons **water**

2 cups **fresh white bread crumbs**

4 **chicken legs** (thighs with drumsticks attached)

**salt** and **pepper**

**Mix** together 3 tablespoons of the oil, 1 teaspoon of the paprika, 1 teaspoon of the oregano, ½ teaspoon of the mustard, ½ teaspoon of the pepper flakes, and some salt in a large bowl. Add the potatoes and toss in the oil mixture until coated.

**Put** the flour on a large plate and mix through the remaining paprika, oregano, mustard, pepper flakes, and season with salt and pepper. Whisk together the eggs and water in a shallow dish and put the bread crumbs on a large plate. Coat the chicken in the flour mixture, then beaten egg, then bread crumbs, until covered.

**Heat** a large roasting pan in a preheated oven, 400°F, for 5 minutes. Meanwhile, heat the remaining oil in a large skillet, add the chicken, and fry on all sides for about 10 minutes until pale golden; do not be tempted to fry for too long because the chicken browns more in the oven. Transfer the chicken to the hot roasting pan, add the potato wedges, and roast for 30–35 minutes until the chicken is cooked through and the potatoes are crisp and golden. Transfer to 4 warm plates and serve with mayonnaise and salad.

**For cheesy fried chicken scallops**, make up the potato wedges as above, then mix the remaining paprika, pepper flakes, and a little salt and pepper with the flour. Take 4 boneless, skinless chicken breasts, about 4 oz each, and using a sharp knife cut horizontally into thin, flat slices about ¼ inch thick. Coat in the flour mixture, then the beaten egg, then in 2 cups fresh white bread crumbs mixed with 2 tablespoons freshly grated Parmesan cheese. Fry in the oil for 10–12 minutes until golden and cooked.

# spinach & potato gratin

Serves **4**

Preparation time **10 minutes**

Cooking time **35 minutes**

1 ¼ lb **potatoes**, peeled and
   thinly sliced

1 lb **spinach leaves**

7 oz **mozzarella cheese**,
   grated

4 **tomatoes**, sliced

3 **eggs**, beaten

1 ¼ cups **whipping cream**

**salt** and **pepper**

**Cook** the potato slices in a large saucepan of salted boiling water for 5 minutes, then drain well.

**Cook** the spinach, meanwhile, in a separate saucepan of boiling water for 1–2 minutes until just wilted. Drain in a colander, then squeeze out the excess water.

**Grease** a large ovenproof dish and line the bottom with half the potato slices. Cover with the spinach and half the mozzarella, seasoning each layer well with salt and pepper. Cover with the remaining potato slices and arrange the tomato slices on top. Sprinkle with the remaining mozzarella.

**Whisk** together the eggs and cream in a bowl and season well with salt and pepper. Pour over the ingredients in the dish.

**Bake** in a preheated oven, 350°F, for about 30 minutes until bubbling and golden. Serve immediately with a salad and crusty bread.

**For tomato, lime, & basil salad**, to serve as an accompaniment, slice or quarter 2 lb tomatoes while the gratin is baking and arrange in a large serving bowl. Sprinkle with ½ red onion, thinly sliced, and a handful of basil leaves. Whisk together 4 tablespoons olive oil, 2 tablespoons chopped basil, 1 tablespoon lime juice, 1 teaspoon grated lime zest, ½ teaspoon honey, 1 crushed garlic clove, and a pinch of cayenne pepper. Season with salt and pepper. Whisk again and pour over the salad. Cover and let stand at room temperature for about 30 minutes, to allow the flavors to mingle. Serve with the gratin.

# cod rarebit

Serves **4**
Preparation time **5 minutes**
Cooking time **15 minutes**

2 tablespoons **whole grain mustard**
3 tablespoons **English beer** or **milk**
2½ cups **cheddar cheese**, grated
2 tablespoons **olive oil**
4 pieces of **cod fillet**, about 7 oz each, pin-boned
**salt** and **pepper**

**Mix** together the mustard, beer or milk, and cheese in a small saucepan. Allow the cheese to melt over a low heat. Stir occasionally and do not allow the mixture to boil, as the cheese will curdle. Remove the pan from the heat and allow to cool and thicken.

**Put** the oil in a skillet over a high heat. Season the fish with salt and pepper, then carefully place into the pan, skin side down. Pan-fry for 4–5 minutes until the skin is crispy, then turn the fish over and cook for a minute more on the other side until the fish is cooked through; be careful not to overcook.

**Spread** the cooled cheese sauce over the fish, and slide the pan under a preheated broiler (keeping the handle away from the heat). Broil for a minute or so until the cheese sauce is bubbling and golden brown.

**For whole grain mustard & cream sauce**, to serve as an accompaniment to the pan-fried cod instead of the rarebit topping, put 2 finely chopped shallots, 1 crushed garlic clove, and a little olive oil in a small saucepan over a low heat. Gently sweat the shallots and garlic for a few minutes until soft and translucent. Pour in ½ cup chicken stock and ¾ cup heavy cream, and bring to a boil. Stir in 1 tablespoon whole grain mustard and serve hot poured over the pan-fried cod.

# toad in the hole

Serves **4**
Preparation time **10 minutes**
Cooking time **25 minutes**

1 cup **all-purpose flour**
1 **egg**
1¼ cups **milk** or equal mixture
  of **milk** and **water**
1 lb good-quality **pork**
  **sausages**
8 **rindless bacon slices**
2 tablespoons **vegetable oil**
**salt** and **pepper**

**Put** the flour and a dash of salt and pepper in a bowl, then crack in the egg. Slowly whisk in the milk or milk-and-water mixture until the batter is smooth and frothy.

**Separate** the sausages from each other. Stretch each slice of bacon by laying it on a cutting board and running the flat edge of a knife along the slice until it is half as long again. Wrap a slice of bacon around each sausage.

**Pour** the oil into a roasting tin and add the bacon-wrapped sausages, keeping them spaced apart. Roast in a preheated oven, 425°F, for 5 minutes until sizzling. Whisk the batter again.

**Take** the roasting pan out of the oven and quickly pour in the batter, making sure that the sausages are still spaced apart. Return the pan to the oven and cook for about 20 minutes until the batter is risen and golden and the sausages are cooked through. Delicious with baked beans and mashed potatoes.

**For vegetarian toad in the hole**, make up the batter as above, adding a large pinch of dried mixed herbs. Cook 8 vegetarian sausages and 2 small red onions, cut into wedges, in 2 tablespoons hot oil in the roasting pan as above. Pour over the batter and continue as above.

# vegetable samosas

Makes **12**
Preparation time **10 minutes**
Cooking time **15–20 minutes**

3 large **potatoes**, boiled,
  peeled, and roughly mashed
2/3 cup **cooked green peas**
1 teaspoon **cumin seeds**
1 teaspoon **amchoor** (dried
  mango powder)
2 **fresh green chilies**, seeded
  and finely chopped
1 small **red onion**, finely
  chopped
3 tablespoons chopped **fresh
  cilantro leaves**
1 tablespoon **mint**, chopped
4 tablespoons **lemon juice**
12 **phyllo pastry sheets**,
  about 12 x 7 inches each
1/2 cup **butter**, melted, for
  brushing
**salt** and **pepper**

**Mix** together the potatoes, peas, cumin seeds, amchoor, chilies, onion, cilantro, mint, and lemon juice in a large bowl. Add a dash of salt and pepper.

**Fold** each sheet of phyllo pastry in half lengthwise. It is best to work with 1 sheet of phyllo at a time; keep the other sheets covered with a slightly damp dish towel or plastic wrap while you work, to prevent them from drying out. Brush the first pastry sheet with a little melted butter. Put a large spoonful of the potato mixture at one end, then fold the corner of the pastry over the mixture, covering it to make a triangular shape. Brush with a little more butter if needed. Continue folding over the triangle of pastry along the length of the pastry strip to make a neat triangular samosa.

**Make** 11 more samosas in the same way, dividing the mixture evenly and brushing the pastry with a little melted butter as you go.

**Arrange** the samosas side by side on a baking sheet, brush with melted butter, and bake in a preheated oven, 400°F, for 15–20 minutes until golden. Serve hot.

# burritos with pork stuffing

Serves **4**

Preparation time **20 minutes**

Cooking time **90 minutes**,
  plus resting

2 lb **boneless rolled pork
  shoulder**

1 tablespoon **vegetable oil**

1 ½ cups **chicken stock**

4 tablespoons **tomato paste**

½ teaspoon grated
  **orange zest**

1 teaspoon **dried red pepper
  flakes**

8 **soft flour tortillas**

**salt**

**Topping**

**sour cream**

½ **avocado**, halved, pitted,
  peeled, and chopped

1 teaspoon **dried red pepper
  flakes**

**Put** the pork in a roasting pan and brush with a little oil. Sprinkle with salt and roast in a preheated oven, 400°F, for 30 minutes. Reduce the oven temperature to 350°F, and roast for another 1 hour or until crisp and golden. Test to make sure that the pork is cooked through by inserting a skewer into the meat—the juices should run clear. Set aside in a warm place, covered with foil, for 15 minutes.

**Make** the sauce, meanwhile. Pour the stock into a saucepan. Add the tomato paste, orange zest, and pepper flakes. Bring to a boil, then reduce the heat and simmer for about 30 minutes until the sauce is thick.

**Take** off the crackling from the roast pork using a sharp knife and cut into strips. Next, cut away any fat on the pork and discard. Tear the meat into shreds. Add the shredded pork to the sauce and heat over low heat.

**Pop** the tortillas in the oven for a couple of minutes to warm and soften (don't let them become dried out and crisp, or you will not be able to roll them properly). Put a little of the pork mixture in the center of each warm tortilla and roll them up. Dollop sour cream on top of the burritos, then pile on the avocado and sprinkle pepper flakes over the top. Serve with the crackling, if you wish.

**For speedy burritos with chicken stuffing**, make the sauce as above. While this reduces down, thinly slice 1 ¼ lb boneless, skinless chicken breasts. Fry in 2 tablespoons vegetable oil for 10 minutes, turning until golden. Add 1 ½ cups chicken stock to the tomato sauce for the last 10 minutes of cooking. Serve with wraps, cream and avocado.

# onion rings in beer batter

Serves **4**
Preparation time **10 minutes**
Cooking time **10 minutes**

4 large **onions**
**vegetable oil**, for deep-frying

**Batter**
1 **egg**, separated
1 tablespoon **olive oil**
½ cup **light beer** such as
 lager, chilled
½ cup **all-purpose flour**
**salt** and **pepper**

**Slice** the onions into ¼ inch thick rings and separate out. Keep the larger rings and ditch the rest, or keep to fry up the next day for breakfast.

**Make** the batter next. Whisk together the egg yolk, oil, beer, and flour in a bowl. Season with salt and pepper. In another clean, dry bowl, whisk the egg white until stiff, then gently fold into the batter until smooth and combined.

**Heat** 2 inches of vegetable oil in a deep heavy saucepan or a deep-fat fryer to 350°–375°F, or until a cube of bread dropped into the oil browns in 30 seconds.

**Dip** the onion rings, a few at a time, into the batter, then carefully drop into the oil and deep-fry in batches for 1–2 minutes until golden. Remove very carefully using a slotted spoon and drain on paper towels. Serve at once with mayonnaise, while the onions are crisp and piping hot.

**For mushrooms in beer batter**, wipe 1 lb button mushrooms with paper towels and dip in the batter. Deep-fry as above, then serve immediately with ²/₃ cup mayonnaise flavored with 2 chopped garlic cloves.

# minty lamb kebabs

Serves **4**

Preparation time **10 minutes**,
  plus marinating and soaking

Cooking time **8–10 minutes**

²/₃ cup **low-fat plain yogurt**

1 **garlic clove**, crushed

2 tablespoons chopped **mint**

1 tablespoon **mint sauce**

12 oz **lean boneless lamb**,
  cubed

2 small **red** or **white onions**,
  cut into wedges

1 **green bell pepper**, cored,
  seeded, and cut into wedges

**To serve**
**green salad**
**couscous**
**lemon wedges** (optional)

**Soak** 8 wooden skewers in cold water for at least
30 minutes, to prevent them burning while the kebabs
are cooking; if using metal skewers, you can leave
out this step, of course.

**Mix** together the yogurt, garlic, mint, and mint sauce
in a bowl. Add the lamb and stir well. Cover and let
marinate in a cool place for 10 minutes or preferably in
the refrigerator for at least 1 hour, to allow the meat to
absorb more of the flavors.

**Thread** the lamb and onion and green pepper wedges
alternately onto the wooden or metal skewers (metal
skewers help the meat to cook right through), arrange
on a broiler rack and cook under a preheated medium-
hot broiler for 8–10 minutes, turning once, until the
meat is cooked through and the onions and peppers are
softened and starting to brown. Alternatively, broiler the
skewers in a preheated griddle pan or over a barbecue.

**Serve** hot with green salad, couscous and lemon
wedges, if desired.

**For curried lamb kebabs**, mix the yogurt with
1 tablespoon mild curry paste, 1 tablespoon mango
chutney, and 1 chopped garlic clove. Marinate the
lamb as above, thread onto the skewers alternately
with the onions and green pepper, broiler as above and
serve with rice.

# healthy eats

# chorizo, pepper, & oregano salad

Serves **2–4**
Preparation time **15 minutes**
Cooking time **15 minutes**

7 oz **chorizo sausage**
1 tablespoon **olive oil**
2 **red bell peppers**, cored, seeded, and cut into ¾ inch squares
2 **yellow bell peppers**, cored, seeded, and cut into ¾ inch squares
1 **red onion**, finely diced
2 tablespoons **sherry vinegar**
½ bunch of **oregano**, roughly chopped
2 cups **arugula**
**salt** and **pepper**

**Peel** off the outer wrapping, or 'skin,' on the chorizo sausage. Cut the sausage into thick slices. Set aside.

**Put** the oil in a large skillet pan over a high heat, add the red and yellow peppers, and cook for 2–3 minutes until they start to brown. Add the chorizo and fry for another 3 minutes, then reduce the heat to low and add the onion. Cook for 3 minutes more until the onion is soft and translucent.

**Deglaze** the pan with the sherry vinegar, scraping up any bits on the bottom with a wooden spoon, and reduce for 1 minute.

**Transfer** the contents of the pan to a large salad bowl and allow to cool slightly. Toss gently with the oregano and arugula. Season with salt and pepper and serve with Romesco Sauce (see below).

**For romesco sauce**, to serve as an accompaniment, soak 1 ancho chili in a bowl of cold water for 1 hour; drain. Put the ancho chili, 4 ready-marinated red bell peppers, 2 peeled and seeded tomatoes, 2 tablespoons blanched toasted almonds, 2 tablespoons toasted hazelnuts, 1 garlic clove, 1 tablespoon red wine vinegar, and 1 teaspoon smoked paprika into a food processor or blender. Whiz briefly to make a smooth sauce. Season with salt and pepper and serve with the salad.

# spicy apple & potato soup

Serves **4**
Preparation time **15 minutes**
Cooking time **30 minutes**

¼ cup **butter**
1 small **onion**, chopped
2 **dessert apples**, peeled,
  cored, and sliced
pinch of **cayenne pepper**
  (or to taste), plus extra
  for sprinking
2½ cups **vegetable stock**
10 oz **floury potatoes**, sliced
1¼ cups **hot milk**
**salt**

**Apple garnish**
1 tablespoon **butter**
½–1 **dessert apple**, peeled,
  cored, and diced

**Melt** the butter in a large heavy saucepan over
a medium heat. Add the onion and cook for 5 minutes
or until softened. Add the apples and cayenne and
cook, stirring, for another 2 minutes.

**Pour** in the stock, then add the potatoes. Bring to
a boil, then reduce the heat and simmer gently for
15–18 minutes until the apples and potatoes are
very tender.

**Blend** the soup in batches in a blender or food
processor until very smooth, then transfer to a clean
saucepan. Reheat gently and stir in the hot milk. Taste
and adjust the seasoning if necessary.

**Make** the apple garnish, meanwhile. Melt the butter
in a small skillet, add the diced apple, and cook over a
high heat until crisp.

**Serve** the soup in warm bowls, garnishing each portion
with some diced apple and a sprinkling of cayenne.

**For spicy apple & parsnip soup**, fry the onion and
apples as above, omitting the cayenne. Add ½ teaspoon
ground turmeric and 1 teaspoon ground cilantro and
stir through to coat the apple and onion mixture in the
spices. Pour in 2½ cups chicken or vegetable stock,
then add 10 oz diced parsnips instead of the potatoes.
Season with salt and black pepper. Continue the recipe
as above.

# shrimp & cranberry salad

Serves **4**

Preparation time **15 minutes**, plus cooling

Cooking time **up to 30 minutes**

1 cup shelled **fresh cranberry beans** (about 1 lb in the pod) or 14 oz can **cranberry beans**, rinsed, and drained

2 tablespoons **extra virgin olive oil**

2 **garlic cloves**, crushed

1 **fresh red chili**, seeded and finely chopped

2 **celery sticks**, thinly sliced

7 oz **cooked peeled shrimp**, tails left on

grated zest and juice of 1 **lemon**

1¼ cups **wild arugula**

**salt**

**Tip** the fresh cranberry beans, if using, into a saucepan. Add enough cold water to cover by about 2 inches and bring to a boil. Skim off any scum that rises to the surface, then reduce the heat to a simmer and cook, uncovered, for 30 minutes or until tender; drain. If using canned beans, simply rinse under cold running water before using, then heat gently in a saucepan over a medium heat for 3 minutes.

**Put** the oil, garlic, and chili in a large bowl. Stir in the warm beans and the celery and season with salt. Allow the salad to cool to room temperature. You can then cover and store in the refrigerator for up to 1 day.

**Allow** the beans to return to room temperature before serving if you have prepared them in advance. Stir in the shrimp and lemon zest and juice, then gently toss through with the arugula or sprinkle on top. Serve at once.

**For sardine, pea, & cranberry bean salad**, prepare and cool the cranberry beans as above, then toss with the lemon zest and juice, omitting the shrimp and arugula. Add 2 x 3¾ oz cans sardines in tomato sauce, a 2 inch piece of diced cucumber, 4 chopped scallions, and ⅔ cup just-cooked frozen peas and gently toss through. Serve on a bed of torn iceberg lettuce leaves.

# malaysian coconut vegetables

Serves **4**

Preparation time **15 minutes**, plus soaking

Cooking time **20 minutes**

²/₃ cup **broccoli florets**

²/₃ cup **green beans**, cut into 1 inch lengths

1 **red bell pepper**, cored, seeded, and sliced

²/₃ cup **zucchini**, thinly sliced

**Coconut sauce**

1 oz **tamarind pulp**

²/₃ cup **boiling water**

1¾ cups **coconut milk**

2 teaspoons **Thai green curry paste**

1 teaspoon grated **fresh ginger root**

1 **onion**, cut into small cubes

½ teaspoon **ground turmeric**

**salt**

**Make** the coconut sauce. Put the tamarind in a bowl. Pour over the measurement water and allow to soak for 30 minutes. Mash the tamarind in the water, then push through a strainer set over another bowl, squashing the tamarind so that you get as much of the pulp as possible; discard the stringy bits and any seeds.

**Take** 2 tablespoons of the cream from the top of the coconut milk and pour it into a wok or large skillet. Add the curry paste, ginger, onion, and turmeric, and cook over a gentle heat, stirring, for 2–3 minutes. Stir in the rest of the coconut milk and the tamarind water. Bring to a boil, then reduce the heat to a simmer and add a pinch of salt.

**Add** the broccoli to the coconut sauce and cook for 5 minutes, then add the green beans and red pepper. Cook, stirring, for another 5 minutes. Finally, stir in the zucchini and cook gently for 1–2 minutes until the zucchini is just tender. Serve immediately with some crispy shrimp crackers.

**For chicken & green beans in coconut sauce**, soak the tamarind and make the coconut sauce as above. Add 1 lb diced boneless, skinless chicken breast to the wok or skillet. Simmer for 5 minutes, then add the sliced green beans, omitting the red pepper and zucchini. Simmer gently for another 5 minutes until the chicken is cooked through. Serve with noodles.

# tuna with green beans & broccoli

Serves **4**
Preparation time **8 minutes**
Cooking time **15 minutes**

1 lb **new potatoes**, scrubbed
8 oz **fine green beans**,
  topped and tailed
7 oz **tenderstem broccoli**
4 **fresh tuna steaks**, about
  6 oz each
1 tablespoon **olive oil**
1/3 cup **toasted hazelnuts**,
  roughly chopped
**salt** and **pepper**

**Dressing**
4 tablespoons **hazelnut oil**
1 tablespoon **lemon juice**
1 teaspoon **Dijon mustard**

**Cook** the potatoes in a saucepan of lightly salted boiling water for 10–15 minutes (depending on the size of the potatoes) until just tender. Drain and allow to cool slightly.

**Meanwhile** cook the beans and broccoli in 2 separate pans of fresh lightly salted boiling water until tender, but still with a slight bite. The green beans will take 4–5 minutes and the broccoli about 3 minutes; be careful not to overcook. Drain the beans and broccoli as soon as they are ready, then tip immediately into ice water to stop the cooking process. Drain again. Cut the cooled potatoes into quarters lengthwise. Set aside.

**Whisk** together all the dressing ingredients in a small bowl (or put them in a screw-top jar with a tight-fitting lid and shake vigorously) and season.

**Heat** a griddle pan over a very high heat. Season the tuna steaks with salt and pepper, and rub with the olive oil. Carefully place in the pan and sear for 1 minute on each side (or longer if the steaks are thickly cut or you want your tuna cooked through, rather than pink).

**Put** the potatoes, beans, and broccoli in a large bowl or serving dish. Add the dressing and toss through gently. Sprinkle with the hazelnuts and serve with the tuna.

**For Asian green beans**, to serve as an alternative accompaniment, mix together 1 tablespoon sesame oil, 2 teaspoons light soy sauce, 1 seeded and finely chopped fresh red chili, 1 teaspoon honey, and 1 tablespoon chopped fresh cilantro. Cook 1 lb topped and tailed green beans in salted boiling water as above. Drain and, while warm, toss in the dressing.

# griddled summer chicken salad

Serves **4**
Preparation time **15 minutes**
Cooking time **45 minutes**

4 **boneless, skinless chicken breasts**, about 4 oz each
2 small **red onions**
2 **red bell peppers**, cored, seeded, and cut into flat pieces
1 bunch of **fresh asparagus**, trimmed
7 oz **new potatoes**, scrubbed, boiled until tender, and halved lengthwise
1 bunch of **basil**
5 tablespoons **olive oil**
2 tablespoons **balsamic vinegar**
**salt** and **pepper**

**Heat** a griddle pan (or ordinary skillet) over a medium-high heat. Place the chicken breasts in the pan and cook for 8–10 minutes on each side. If you are using a griddle pan, cook the chicken on each side without moving it in the pan, so that it ends up with a distinct striped pattern; if you desire, change the position of the chicken halfway through cooking on each side, to end up with crisscross markings. When cooked, remove from the pan and cut roughly into chunks. Set aside.

**Cut** the red onions into wedges, keeping the root ends intact to hold the wedges together. Arrange in the pan and grill for 5 minutes on each side until softened and starting to brown. Remove from the pan and set aside. Place the flat pieces of red pepper in the pan, skin side down, and grill for 8 minutes on the skin side only, so that the skins are charred. Remove, set aside, then grill the asparagus in the pan for 6 minutes, turning often.

**Put** the boiled potatoes in a large bowl. Tear the basil, keeping a few leaves intact to garnish. Add the torn leaves to the bowl, with the chicken, onions, red pepper, and asparagus. Add the olive oil and balsamic vinegar, and season. Toss the salad, season with salt and pepper, and garnish with the reserved basil and serve.

**For summer chicken wraps**, omit the potatoes and make the recipe as above. Warm 4 soft flour tortillas, then spread with ¾ cup hummus. Toss the griddled chicken, cut into strips, and the pan-grilled vegetables with 2 tablespoons olive oil, 2 tablespoons balsamic vinegar, and a few basil leaves. Divide among the tortillas, then roll up tightly and serve, cut in half crosswise, while the chicken is still warm.

# fragrant tofu & noodle soup

Serves **2**

Preparation time **15 minutes**, plus draining

Cooking time **10 minutes**

4 oz **firm tofu**, diced

1 tablespoon **sesame oil**

3 oz **fine dried rice noodles**

2½ cups **vegetable stock**

1 inch piece of **fresh ginger root**, peeled and thickly sliced

1 large **garlic clove**, thickly sliced

3 **kaffir lime leaves**, torn in half

2 **lemon grass stalks**, tough outer layers removed, halved

handful of **spinach** or **bok choy leaves**

½ cup **bean sprouts**

1–2 **fresh red chilies**, seeded and thinly sliced

2 tablespoons roughly chopped **fresh cilantro**

1 tablespoon **Thai fish sauce**

**Put** the tofu on a plate covered with paper towels. Allow to stand for 10 minutes to drain.

**Heat** the sesame oil in a wok or large nonstick skillet until hot, add the tofu, and stir-fry for 2–3 minutes until golden brown. Remove with a slotted spoon and drain on paper towels.

**Meanwhile,** soak the rice noodles in a saucepan of boiling water for 2 minutes, then drain well.

**Pour** the stock into a large heavy saucepan. Add the ginger, garlic, lime leaves, and lemon grass and bring to a boil. Reduce the heat, add the tofu, drained noodles, spinach or bok choy, bean sprouts, and chilies and heat through for 2 minutes.

**Stir** in the cilantro and fish sauce, then pour into warm deep soup bowls. Serve hot with lime wedges and chili sauce if liked.

**For Thai shrimp & noodle soup**, omit the tofu and soak and drain the noodles as above. Pour the vegetable stock into a saucepan and add the ginger, garlic, and 2 teaspoons Thai green curry paste. Bring to a boil. Add 4 oz thawed small frozen shrimp and the drained noodles, spinach or bok choy, bean sprouts, and chilies. Cook until the shrimp are piping hot, then mix in the chopped cilantro and serve.

# beef, pumpkin, & ginger stew

Serves **6**
Preparation time **20 minutes**
Cooking time **1½ hours**

2 tablespoons **all-purpose flour**
1½ lb **lean stewing beef**, diced
2 tablespoons **butter**
3 tablespoons **vegetable oil**
1 **onion**, chopped
2 **carrots**, sliced
2 **parsnips**, sliced
3 **bay leaves**
several **thyme sprigs**
2 tablespoons **tomato paste**
1¼ lb **pumpkin**, peeled, seeded, and cut into small chunks
1 tablespoon **dark muscovado sugar**
¼ cup **fresh ginger root**, peeled and finely chopped
small handful of **flat-leaf parsley**, chopped, plus extra to garnish
**salt** and **pepper**

**Season** the flour with salt and pepper and use to coat the beef. Melt the butter with the oil in a large saucepan over a medium-high heat. When the butter is foaming, fry the meat in 2 batches until browned all over, draining with a slotted spoon. Set aside on a plate.

**Reduce** the heat, add the onion, carrots and parsnips to the saucepan and fry gently for 5 minutes until softened but not browned.

**Return** the meat to the pan and add the bay leaves, thyme, and tomato paste. Pour in just enough water to cover the ingredients and bring slowly to a boil. Reduce the heat to its lowest setting, cover, and simmer very gently for 45 minutes.

**Add** the pumpkin, sugar, ginger, and parsley and simmer gently for an additional 30 minutes until the pumpkin is soft and the meat is tender. Check the seasoning, adding salt and pepper if needed, and serve sprinkled with extra parsley.

**For beef, sweet potato, & horseradish stew**, cook the recipe as above, replacing the pumpkin with 1 lb sweet potatoes, cut into chunks, and the ginger with 3 tablespoons hot horseradish sauce.

# mackerel & wild rice niçoise

Serves **3–4**
Preparation time **20 minutes**,
  plus cooling
Cooking time **25 minutes**

½ cup **wild rice**
1 cup **green beans**, topped
  and tailed, then halved
10 oz large **mackerel fillets**,
  pin-boned
6 tablespoons **olive oil**
12 **black olives**
8 **canned anchovy fillets**,
  drained and halved
1 cup **cherry tomatoes**,
  halved
3 **hard-cooked eggs**, cut into
  quarters
1 tablespoon **lemon juice**
1 tablespoon **French mustard**
2 tablespoons chopped
  **chives**
**salt** and **pepper**

**Cook** the rice in plenty of boiling water for 20–25 minutes until tender. (The grains will start to split open when they are just cooked.) Add the green beans and cook for another 2 minutes.

**Lay** the mackerel, skin side up, on a foil-lined broiler rack, while the rice is cooking. Brush with 1 tablespoon of the oil and cook under a preheated medium-hot broiler for 8–10 minutes, turning after the first 5 minutes, until cooked through; the second side should not take as long to cook as the first. Allow to cool.

**Drain** the rice and beans and mix together in a salad bowl with the olives, anchovies, tomatoes, and eggs. Flake the mackerel, discarding any stray bones, and add to the bowl.

**Whisk** the remaining oil with the lemon juice, mustard, and chives in a small bowl, and season with a little salt and pepper. Add to the bowl.

**Toss** the ingredients together lightly, cover, and chill until ready to serve.

**For fresh tuna & wild rice niçoise**, replace the mackerel with 7 oz fresh tuna steaks, frying them in a little olive oil for 2–3 minutes on each side so that they are just pink in the center. Continue the recipe as above.

# grilled vegetable & haloumi salad

Serves **4**
Preparation time **15 minutes**
Cooking time **25 minutes**

12 **cherry tomatoes on the
vine**
4 **portobello mushrooms**
**olive oil**
2 **zucchini**, cut into
batons about 1 ½ x ¾ inches
1 lb **fresh asparagus**, trimmed
8 oz **haloumi cheese**, cut into
¼ inch slices
**salt** and **pepper**

**Dressing**
2 tablespoons **olive oil**
2 tablespoons **balsamic
vinegar**

**Put** the tomatoes and mushrooms in a roasting pan, drizzle with about 2 tablespoons oil, season with salt and pepper, and cook in a preheated oven, 350°F, for 10 minutes.

**Put** the zucchini and asparagus in a large bowl, meanwhile. Drizzle with olive oil and a pinch of salt and pepper. Heat a griddle pan over a high heat, and grill the asparagus and zucchini until starting to brown. Transfer the asparagus and zucchini to the oven with the tomatoes and mushrooms and cook for 6–8 minutes.

**Use** a piece of paper towels to wipe the griddle pan clean. Pat the cheese slices dry with paper towels. Heat 1 teaspoon olive oil in the pan over a medium heat. Grill the haloumi, turning once (use a spatula to loosen the cheese first), for about 4 minutes until lightly golden with grill marks on both sides. Make the dressing by whisking together the oil and vinegar. Stack the grilled vegetables and mushrooms on 4 warm plates, dividing the ingredients evenly. Top with slices of cheese, spoon over the dressing, and serve immediately.

**For watermelon & haloumi cheese**, cut 8 oz haloumi cheese into thin slices. Heat 1 tablespoon olive oil in a large nonstick skillet over a medium heat and cook the cheese for about 4 minutes until golden and crispy on both sides. Drain and pat dry with paper towels. Halve, peel, and seed ½ small watermelon and cut the flesh into small triangles. Toss the melon with a small bunch of chopped mint and the diced flesh of 1 ripe halved, pitted and peeled avocado. Serve with the grilled haloumi.

# turkey & orange stir-fry

Serves **4**
Preparation time **30 minutes**,
  plus marinating
Cooking time **10 minutes**

12 oz **boneless, skinless
  turkey breast**, cut into large
  chunks or strips
grated zest and juice of
  **2 oranges**
1 tablespoon **cornstarch**
1 tablespoon **vegetable oil**
½ **red bell pepper**, cored,
  seeded, and cut into strips
½ **green bell pepper**, cored,
  seeded, and cut into strips
3 **celery sticks**, cut into cubes
1 large **carrot**, cut into thin
  slices
**salt** and **pepper**

**Marinade**
1 tablespoon **light soy sauce**
2 tablespoons **orange juice**

**Make** the marinade first. Mix together the soy sauce
and orange juice in a bowl or shallow dish. Add the
turkey to the marinade, cover with plastic wrap and
allow to marinate in the refrigerator for 30 minutes.

**Mix** the orange juice with enough water to make
²/₃ cup. Add the cornstarch and season with a dash of
salt and pepper. Stir until the cornstarch has dissolved,
then set aside.

**Remove** the turkey from the marinade with a slotted
spoon, and put on a plate. Keep the marinade.

**Heat** the oil in a wok or large skillet over a medium-high
heat. Add the turkey and stir-fry for 4–5 minutes, then
add the orange zest, red and green peppers, celery, and
carrot. Stir-fry for another 3 minutes.

**Stir** the cornstarch mixture, then add it and the reserved
marinade to the wok or skillet. Bring to a boil, and stir
well for a minute or so until the sauce starts to thicken
and becomes glossy. Serve immediately on a mound of
boiled rice.

**For turkey & mixed vegetable stir-fry**, marinate the
turkey and make up the orange sauce as above.
Stir-fry the turkey until just cooked through, then
add 9 oz of ready-prepared stir-fry vegetables and
2 chopped garlic cloves. Stir-fry for 2–3 minutes, pour
in the orange sauce and marinade, and cook until the
sauce has thickened.

# kale soup with garlic croutons

Serves **8**
Preparation time **25 minutes**
Cooking time **45 minutes**

¼ cup **butter**
1 **onion**, chopped
2 **carrots**, sliced
1 lb **kale**, tough stalks
   discarded
5 cups **water**
2½ cups **vegetable stock**
1 tablespoon **lemon juice**
10 oz **potatoes**, sliced
pinch of grated **nutmeg**
**salt** and **pepper**
2 **kale leaves**, thinly shredded,
   to garnish

**Garlic croutons**
6–8 tablespoons **olive oil**
3 **garlic cloves**, sliced
6–8 slices **whole-wheat
   bread,** crusts removed, cut
   into ½ inch cubes

**Melt** the butter in a large saucepan, add the onion, and cook over a medium heat for 5 minutes or until soft. Add the carrots and kale in batches, stirring constantly. Cook for 2 minutes until the kale has just wilted.

**Pour** in the measurement water and stock, then add the lemon juice, potatoes, and nutmeg. Season with salt and pepper. Bring to a boil, then reduce the heat, cover, and simmer for 30–35 minutes until all the vegetables are tender. Add a little water if the soup is too thick.

**Make** the croutons while the soup is cooking. Heat the oil in a large skillet, add the garlic, and cook over a medium heat for 1 minute. Add the bread cubes and cook, turning frequently, until golden brown. Remove with a slotted spoon and drain on paper towels. Remove and discard the garlic. Add the shredded kale to the pan and cook, stirring constantly, until crispy.

**Reheat** the soup gently. Serve in warm soup bowls, garnished with the croutons and crispy shredded kale.

**For caldo verde**, heat 2 tablespoons olive oil in a pan. Add 2 chopped onions, 4 oz diced chorizo sausage, and fry over a medium heat until golden. Add the carrots and kale as above, mixing in 2 chopped garlic cloves and 1 teaspoon smoked paprika, taking care that the paprika does not burn and turn bitter. Continue the recipe as above.

# beets, spinach, & orange salad

Serves **4**

Preparation time **20 minutes**, plus cooling

Cooking time **1–2 hours**

1 lb **uncooked beets,** preferably of a similar size

2 **garlic cloves**, peeled but left whole

handful of **oregano leaves**

1 teaspoon **vegetable oil**

1 tablespoon **balsamic vinegar**

4 cups **baby spinach**

2 **oranges**, peeled, any white pith removed and cut into segments

**salt** and **pepper**

**Vinaigrette**

1 tablespoon **balsamic vinegar**

1 teaspoon **Dijon mustard**

4 tablespoons **olive oil**

pinch of **sugar** (optional)

**Put** the whole beets in the center of a large piece of foil, along with the garlic and oregano. Sprinkle with pepper and drizzle over the vegetable oil and vinegar. Gather up the foil loosely and fold over at the top to seal it. Place on a baking sheet and bake in a preheated oven, 400°F, for 1–2 hours (depending on how large the beets are) until tender.

**Unwrap** the foil parcel and allow the beets to cool before peeling and slicing them. Discard the garlic. Make the vinaigrette. Mix together the balsamic vinegar and mustard in a small bowl. Season with a little salt and pepper. Gradually add the olive oil, whisking constantly, until smooth and well combined. Taste and adjust the seasoning as needed, adding a pinch of sugar to reduce the acidity, if desired, bearing in mind the sweetness of the roasted beets. Whisk again until the sugar has dissolved. Alternatively, put all the vinaigrette ingredients in a screw-top jar, seal tightly, and shake vigorously until well combined.

**Put** the spinach in a large bowl, and gently toss together with beets and orange. Drizzle over the vinaigrette, sprinkle with pepper, and enjoy.

**For beetroot, spinach, & goat cheese salad**, prepare and roast the beets as above. Cool, peel, and slice, then put in a salad bowl with the spinach and vinaigrette dressing. Lightly toast 4 slices ciabatta or French bread on both sides under a preheated broiler. Cut a 4 oz goat cheese into 4 slices and arrange on top of the toasted bread. Cook under the hot broiler for a few minutes until the cheese has melted, then serve on a bed of salad.

# griddled chicken fajitas

Serves **4**

Preparation time **20 minutes**, plus marinating

Cooking time **16–20 minutes**

4 **boneless, skinless chicken breasts**, about 4 oz each

4 ripe **tomatoes**

4 large **soft flour tortillas**

²/₃ cup **sour cream**

1 **avocado**, halved, pitted, peeled, and sliced

4 **scallions**, sliced

½ **red onion**, finely chopped

**tortilla chips**, to serve (optional)

**salt** and **pepper**

**Marinade**

2 tablespoons **light soy sauce**

1¼ inch piece of **fresh ginger root**, peeled and finely chopped

2 **garlic cloves**, finely chopped

2 tablespoons **olive oil**

1 bunch of **fresh cilantro**, chopped

1 **fresh red chili**, seeded and chopped

2 tablespoons **lime juice**

**Combine** all the ingredients for the marinade in a shallow dish. Add the chicken breasts, and allow to marinate at room temperature for 2 hours, or in the refrigerator for 24 hours. Put the tomatoes in a bowl, and pour over boiling water to cover. Leave for 1–2 minutes, then drain, cut a cross at the stem end of each tomato, and peel off the skins. Cut the tomatoes into slices.

**Heat** a griddle pan or ordinary skillet. Place the marinated chicken breasts in the pan and cook for 8–10 minutes on each side. If you are using a griddle pan, cook the chicken on each side without moving it in the pan, so that it ends up with a distinct striped pattern of grill marks; if you desire, change the position of the chicken halfway through cooking on each side, to end up with crisscross markings. When cooked, remove the chicken from the pan and slice into long strips.

**Place** the tortillas under a preheated broiler and cook for 30 seconds on each side until warmed through but not crisp. Spread a spoonful of sour cream over one side of each tortilla, then add a little tomato, avocado, and a sprinkling of scallions and red onion. Arrange the pieces of griddled chicken on top and season with salt and pepper. Roll up each tortilla tightly and cut in half crosswise. Serve with tortilla chips, if desired.

**For guacamole**, to accompany the fajitas, halve and pit 2 ripe avocados. Scoop out the flesh, put in a bowl, and mash with a fork. Mix with the juice of 1 lime, 3 tablespoons chopped fresh cilantro, 1 skinned and finely diced tomato, and, if desired, 1 finely chopped jalapeño chili. Spoon onto the tortillas instead of sour cream.

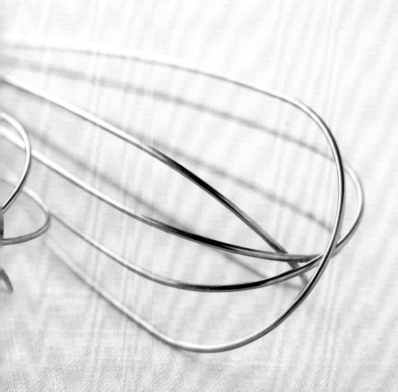

# sweet treats

# easy chocolate fudge cake

Cuts into **12**
Preparation time **10 minutes**,
   plus cooling and setting time
Cooking time **50–55 minutes**

8 oz **bittersweet chocolate**,
   broken into pieces
1 cup **butter**
4 **eggs**, beaten
½ cup **superfine sugar**
2 cups **self-rising flour**, sifted

**Frosting**
6 oz **bittersweet chocolate**,
   broken into pieces
¼ cup **single cream**

**Grease** an 8 x 12 inch baking pan lightly and line with nonstick parchment paper, snipping diagonally into the corners of the paper and pressing it into the pan to line the base and sides. Put the chocolate and butter in a heatproof bowl set over a saucepan of gently simmering water (don't let the bowl touch the water) and stir over a low heat until melted. Allow to cool for 5 minutes.

**Whisk** together the eggs and sugar in a bowl for 5 minutes until thick, while the cake is cooking. Beat in the cooled chocolate mixture and fold in the flour.

**Spoon** the mixture into the prepared tin and bake in a preheated oven, 325°F for 45–50 minutes until risen and firm to the touch. Allow to cool in the tin for 10 minutes, then turn out onto a wire rack to cool completely, removing the paper from the base.

**Make** the frosting, meanwhile. Put the chocolate in a saucepan with the cream and heat gently, stirring, until melted. Allow to cool for 1 hour until thickened to a pouring consistency, then spread over the cake. Allow to set for 30 minutes before serving.

**For fudge cake with chocolate butter frosting**, instead of the ganache icing above, put 1 cup unsalted butter, at room temperature, in a bowl. Gradually beat in 2 cups sifted confectioners' sugar and ½ cup sifted cocoa powder until smooth. Spread over the cooled cake and decorate with 2 oz grated milk chocolate.

# warm summer fruit trifle

Makes **6**
Preparation time **20 minutes**
Cooking time **20 minutes**

8 **lady fingers** or 4 oz **plain
   sponge cake** or **jelly roll**
3 tablespoons **orange juice**
2 cups **frozen mixed summer
   fruits**, just thawed
1 ½ cups **ready-made custard**

**Meringue topping**
3 **egg whites**
¹/₃ cup **granulated sugar**

**Crumble** the lady fingers or cake into the bottom of 6 individual ovenproof dishes. Drizzle the orange juice over the tops, then add the mixed fruits. Dollop the custard over the tops.

**Whisk** the egg whites in a clean, dry bowl until stiff peaks form, then gradually whisk in the sugar, a spoonful at a time, until all the sugar has been added. Keep whisking for another 1–2 minutes until the mixture is thick and glossy.

**Spoon** the meringue mixture over the top of the custard in large swirls. Place the dishes on a baking sheet. Cook in a preheated oven, 325°F, for 20 minutes until the meringue is golden brown on top. Serve warm.

**For chilled summer fruit trifle**, in the bottom of a large bowl, sprinkle the crumbled ladyfingers or sponge cake with 3 tablespoons sherry. Top with the thawed fruits, then the custard. Whip ²/₃ cup heavy cream until it forms soft swirls. Spoon over the top of the trifle instead of the meringue. Chill until ready to serve, then decorate with sugar sprinkles or 4 teaspoons toasted slivered almonds.

# lemon sorbet

Serves **4**

Preparation time **15 minutes**, plus chilling and freezing

½ cup **superfine ugar**

5 tablespoons **boiling water**

2 cups freshly squeezed **lemon juice** (about 10 lemons)

**lemon rind curls**, to decorate (use a zester to make the curls)

**shortbread cookies**, to serve

**Put** the sugar in a heatproof pitcher. Pour over the measurement water and stir until the sugar has started to dissolve. Pour in the lemon juice and stir well until all the sugar has dissolved.

**Pour** the mixture into a shallow freezerproof container and cover with plastic wrap. Chill for 30 minutes.

**Churn** in an ice-cream machine according to the manufacturer's instructions. Alternatively, freeze in the same container, beating the sorbet with a whisk at 45-minute intervals to break up the ice crystals, until almost completely frozen. Process the sorbet in a food processor or blender until smooth. Freeze until solid.

**Transfer** to the refrigerator 10 minutes before serving to soften slightly. Serve in individual bowls or glasses, decorated with lemon rind curls and accompanied by shortbread cookies. The sorbet is best eaten on the day it is made.

**For gin & lemon float**, make up the sorbet as above, stirring in 6 tablespoons gin. Freeze as above. Pour 4 cups carbonated lemonade into glasses, top with scoops of the sorbet, and decorate with slices of lime. Serve immediately with spoons and straws.

# jelly roly-poly

Serves **6**
Preparation time **25 minutes**
Cooking time **2 hours**

2½ cups **self-rising flour**
1 teaspoon **baking powder**
1 cup **shredded vegetable suet**
⅓ cup **superfine sugar**
1 cup **fresh bread crumbs**
finely grated zest of 1 **lemon**
finely grated zest of 1 **orange**
1 **egg**, beaten
⅔ to ¾ cup **milk**
6 tablespoons **raspberry jelly**
1¼ cups **frozen raspberries**, just thawed

**Put** the flour, baking powder, suet, and sugar in a bowl, then stir in the bread crumbs and lemon and orange zests. Add the egg, then gradually mix in enough of the milk to make a soft but not sticky dough.

**Knead** the dough lightly, then roll out to a 12 inch square. Spread with the jelly, leaving a 1 inch border round the edges, then sprinkle the raspberries on top. Brush the border with a little milk, then roll up the pastry. Wrap loosely in nonstick parchment paper, twisting the edges together and leaving space for the pudding to rise, then wrap loosely in foil.

**Put** on a roasting rack set over a large roasting pan, then carefully pour boiling water into the pan but not over the roasting rack (the water must not touch the wrapped pudding). Cover the pan with foil and twist over the edges to seal well. Bake in a preheated oven, 300°F, for 2 hours until the pudding is well risen. Check once or twice during baking and top up the water level if needed. Transfer the pudding to a cutting board using a clean dish towel. Unwrap and discard the parchment paper, cut the roly-poly into thick slices, and serve with hot custard.

**For spotted dick**, warm 3 tablespoons orange juice or rum in a small saucepan. Add 1 cup raisins, 1 teaspoon ground ginger, and ¼ teaspoon grated nutmeg and allow to soak for 1 hour or longer. Add to the flour mixture just before adding the egg and milk. Shape the dough into a long sausage, wrap in nonstick parchment paper and foil, and steam in the oven as above. Serve in thick slices with hot custard flavored with a little extra rum, if desired.

# rum & raisin chocolate brownies

Cuts into **20**

Preparation time **30 minutes**,
  plus soaking

Cooking time **25–30 minutes**

3 tablespoons **white** or
  **dark rum**

²/₃ cup **raisins**

8 oz **bittersweet chocolate**,
  broken into pieces

1 cup **butter**

4 **eggs**

1 scant cup **superfine sugar**

¾ cup **self-rising flour**

1 teaspoon **baking powder**

4 oz **white** or **milk chocolate**

**Warm** the rum gently in a small saucepan. Add the
raisins and allow to soak for 2 hours or overnight.
Heat the dark chocolate and butter gently in a saucepan
until both have just melted, taking care not to scorch
the chocolate.

**Beat** together the eggs and sugar in a bowl using an
electric mixer until the mixture is very thick and the
beaters leaves a trail when lifted above it.

**Fold** the warm chocolate and butter into the beaten
eggs and sugar. Sift the flour and baking powder over
the top, then fold through. Pour the mixture into a lightly
greased 7 x 11 inch roasting pan lined with nonstick
parchment paper and ease into the corners. Spoon the
rum-soaked raisins over the top. Bake in a preheated
oven, 350°F for 25–30 minutes until well risen; the top
should be crusty and cracked and the center still slightly
soft. Allow to cool and harden in the pan.

**Lift** out of the pan using the lining paper. To make the
topping, melt the white or milk chocolate in a heatproof
bowl set over a saucepan of gently simmering water
(don't let the bowl touch the water), then drizzle over
the top of the brownies. Let harden, then cut into 20
even-sized pieces. Peel off and discard the paper. Store
the brownies in an airtight container for up to 3 days.

**For triple chocolate brownies**, omit the rum-soaked
raisins and instead sprinkle 4 oz finely chopped milk
chocolate and 4 oz finely chopped white chocolate over
the mixture just before baking. Bake as above, then
omit the chocolate topping.

# almond angel cakes with berries

Serves **6**
Preparation time **15 minutes**
Cooking time **10–12 minutes**

**4 egg whites**
3 tablespoons **granulated sugar**
½ cup **slivered almonds**
generous pinch of **cream of tartar**
2 tablespoons **slivered almonds**
1 tablespoon sifted **confectioners' sugar**, to dust (optional)

**Berries with yogurt**
¾ cup **plain yogurt**
2 tablespoons **honey** or **sifted confectioners' sugar** (optional)
2 ½ cups **frozen mixed berry fruits**, just thawed

**Brush** 6 cups of a deep muffin pan with a little sunflower oil and line the bases with rounds of waxed paper. Whisk the egg whites in a clean, dry bowl until stiff, moist peaks form. Whisk in the granulated sugar, a teaspoonful at a time, until it has all been added. Keep whisking for 1–2 minutes until thick and glossy.

**Fold** in the ground almonds and cream of tartar, then spoon the mixture into the prepared sections of the muffin pan. Sprinkle the slivered almonds over the top of each one. Bake in a preheated oven, 350°F, for 10–12 minutes until golden brown and set. Carefully loosen the edges of the cakes with a knife, then lift onto a wire rack to cool.

**Put** the yogurt in a bowl and stir through the honey or icing sugar to sweeten, if desired. Swirl the thawed berry fruits through the yogurt. Arrange the angel cakes on a serving plate, dusted with the confectioners' sugar, if desired. Serve with the swirled fruits and yogurt for spooning over.

**For almond meringues**, whisk the 4 egg whites until stiff peaks form, then gradually whisk in 1 cup superfine sugar until all the sugar has dissolved and the mixture is thick and glossy. Fold in ½ cup finely chopped toasted slivered almonds. Scoop dessertspoons of the mixture onto a baking sheet lined with nonstick parchment paper. Cook in a preheated oven, 225°F, for 1 hour or until the meringues lift easily off the paper. Allow to cool in the oven with the door ajar, then remove and cool completely. Sandwich together with 1½ cups whipped heavy cream.

# lemon meringue pie

Serves **6**
Preparation time **40 minutes**,
  plus chilling and standing
Cooking time **35–40 minutes**

12 oz chilled **ready-made**
  or **homemade sweet**
  **shortcrust pastry**
1 scant cup **superfine sugar**
1/3 cup **cornstarch**
grated zest and juice of
  2 **lemons**
4 **eggs**, separated
3/4 cup **water**

**Roll** out the pastry thinly on a lightly floured surface and use to line an 8 inch diameter x 2 inch deep loose-bottomed fluted tart pan, pressing into the sides. Trim the top and prick the bottom of the pie shell with a fork. Chill for 15 minutes, then line with nonstick parchment paper, add macaroni or beans and bake in a preheated oven, 375°F, for 15 minutes more until crisp and golden. Remove the paper and macaroni or beans and bake for a further 5 minutes until crisp and golden.

**Put** 3 oz of the sugar in a bowl with the cornflour and lemon rind. Add the egg yolks and mix until smooth. Make the lemon juice up to 1 1/4 cups with water, pour into a saucepan, and bring to a boil. Gradually mix into the yolk mixture, whisking until smooth. Pour back in the pan and bring to a boil, whisking until very thick. Pour into the pie shell and spread level. Set aside.

**Whisk** the egg whites in a clean, dry bowl until they form stiff peaks. Gradually whisk in the remaining sugar, a teaspoonful at a time, then keep whisking for 1–2 minutes more until thick and glossy. Spoon the meringue mixture over the lemon layer to cover completely and swirl with a spoon. Reduce the oven temperature to 350°F and cook the pie for 15–20 minutes until the meringue is golden and cooked through. Leave for 15 minutes, then carefully remove the tart pan and transfer to a serving plate. Serve warm or cold with cream.

**For citrus meringue pie**, mix the grated zests of 1 lime, 1 lemon, and 1/2 small orange with the cornstarch. Squeeze the juice from the fruits and make up to 1 1/4 cups with water. Continue the recipe as above.

# peanut butter cookies

Makes **32**
Preparation time **10 minutes**
Cooking time **12 minutes**

½ cup **unsalted butter**, at
　room temperature
⅔ cup **brown sugar**
½ cup **crunchy peanut butter**
1 **egg**, lightly beaten
1¼ cups **all-purpose flour**
½ teaspoon **baking powder**
½ cup **unsalted peanuts**

**Beat** together the butter and sugar in a bowl or food processor until pale and creamy. Add the peanut butter, egg, flour, and baking powder and stir together until combined. Stir in the peanuts.

**Drop** large teaspoonfuls of the mixture on to 3 large, lightly oiled baking sheets, leaving 2 inch gaps between each one for them to spread during cooking.

**Flatten** the mounds slightly with a fork and bake in a preheated oven, 375°F, for 12 minutes until golden around the edges. Allow to cool on the baking sheets for 2 minutes, then transfer to a wire rack to cool completely.

**For peanut butter & chocolate chip cookies**, use only ¼ cup unsalted peanuts and add ½ cup milk chocolate chips. Make and bake the cookies as above.

# banoffee pie

Serves **6**
Preparation time **35 minutes**,
   plus chilling and cooling
Cooking time **8 minutes**

1 cup **unsalted butter**
2 tablespoons **corn syrup**
3 cups **crushed graham
   crackers**
½ cup **dark brown sugar**
13 oz can **sweetened
   condensed milk**
1¼ cups **heavy cream**
3 small ripe **bananas**
juice of 1 **lemon**
**bittersweet chocolate**,
   grated, to decorate

**Melt** half the butter and the syrup in a saucepan, add the cracker crumbs and mix well. Tip into a greased 8 inch springform tin and press evenly over the base and up the sides almost to the pan's top. Chill.

**Heat** the remaining butter and the sugar in a nonstick skillet until the butter has melted and the sugar dissolved. Add the condensed milk and cook over a medium heat, stirring continuously, for 4–5 minutes until the mixture thickens and begins to smell of caramel (do not have the heat too high or the condensed milk will burn).

**Remove** the pan from the heat and allow the mixture to cool for 1–2 minutes, then pour into the crumb shell. Allow to cool completely, then chill for at least 1 hour.

**Whip** the cream, just before serving, until soft peaks form. Peel and halve the bananas lengthwise, then cut into slices and toss in the lemon juice. Fold two-thirds of the banana slices into the cream, then spoon over the toffee layer. Arrange the remaining bananas on top. Loosen the edge of the crumb crust with a spatula, then remove the pan and transfer the pie to a serving plate. Sprinkle with grated chocolate and serve cut into slices.

**For banoffee ice cream sundae**, omit the crumb base and make the toffee sauce as above, but cook for just 2 minutes so that it is runnier. Allow to cool. Layer the sliced bananas evenly in 6 serving glasses with 12 scoops vanilla ice cream, 6 crumbled brandy snap cookies and a drizzle of the sauce, reheated if very thick. Sprinkle with chocolate curls or grated chocolate.

# chunky monkeys

Makes **12**
Preparation time **10 minutes**
Cooking time **10–12 minutes**

1¾ cups **all-purpose flour**
1 teaspoon **baking soda**
½ cup **sugar**
½ cup **butter**, cut into cubes
1 **egg**
1 tablespoon **milk**
5 oz **white chocolate**, roughly
  chopped
⅓ cup **candied cherries**,
  roughly chopped

**Put** the flour, baking soda, and sugar in a bowl and mix through. Add the butter and blend with the fingertips until the mixture resembles bread crumbs.

**Beat** together the egg and milk in a separate bowl. Add the chopped chocolate and candied cherries, then mix into the flour mixture and stir well until smooth.

**Drop** heaping spoonfuls of the cookie mixture, well spaced apart, onto a greased baking sheet and bake in a preheated oven, 350°F, for 10–12 minutes until lightly golden. Allow to harden on the sheet for 2 minutes, then slide off onto a wire rack or plate to cool.

**For double chocolate chunky monkeys**, replace 2 tablespoons of the flour with unsweetened cocoa powder. Continue the recipe as above, adding the roughly chopped white chocolate and ½ cup toasted blanched hazelnuts, roughly chopped, instead of the cherries. Bake as above.

# really easy fruit cake

Serves **8**

Preparation time **20 minutes**

Cooking time **1–1¼ hours**

2 cups **self-rising flour**

½ teaspoon **ground mixed spice**

½ teaspoon **ground cinnamon**

½ cup **butter** or **margarine**

½ cup **brown sugar**

¾ cup **currants**

¼ cup **candied cherries**, quartered

1 large **egg**

5 tablespoons **milk**

**Demerara sugar**, for sprinkling (optional)

**Mix** together the flour, mixed spice, and cinnamon in a large bowl. Add the butter and blend with your fingertips until the mixture resembles bread crumbs. Stir in the sugar, currants, and candied cherries.

**Whisk** together the egg and milk in a separate bowl, add to the fruit mixture, and beat thoroughly.

**Pour** the mixture into a greased 8 inch square cake pan lined with nonstick parchment paper. Sprinkle the top with a little Demerara sugar, if desired. Bake in a preheated oven, 350°F, for 1–1¼ hours until the top is firm but springy to the touch; a skewer inserted into the center of the cake should come out clean. Allow to stand in the pan for a few minutes, then turn out onto a wire rack to cool completely. Cut into squares to serve.

**For fruited date & orange cake**, make up the spiced crumb mixture as above, then stir in the grated zest of 1 orange and 1 cup chopped ready-to-eat dates. Stir in the egg and milk mixture, spoon into the prepared pan, and cook as above.

# raspberry mallow fondue

Serves **4**
Preparation time **5 minutes**
Cooking time **10 minutes**

2 cups **raspberries**
2 cups **marshmallows**
²/₃ cup **double cream**
few drops of **lemon juice**

**To serve**
**raspberries**, **marshmallows**
  and **shortbread cookies**,
  for dipping

**Puree** the raspberries in a blender or food processor until smooth, or rub through a strainer into a bowl.

**Put** the puréed raspberries, marshmallows, and cream in a fondue pot and melt over a low heat, stirring constantly. Add the lemon juice and heat through, but do not allow to boil.

**Move** the fondue pot to the table and keep warm on a burner, then gather all your friends around and dip the cookies, raspberries, and marshmallows into the raspberry mallow, while still warm.

**For peach mallow fondue**, make a cross cut in 1 large ripe peach, put in a bowl, cover with boiling water, and leave for 1 minute. Drain and peel off the skin. Cut the peach in half, remove and discard the pit and roughly chop the flesh. Purée in a blender or food processor until smooth, or rub through a strainer. Heat with the marshmallows and cream as above. Serve with peach slices and cookies as above.

# chocolate overload

Serves **4**
Preparation time **8 minutes**

8 **chocolate cream sandwich
cookies**, crushed
2 tablespoons **butter**, melted
2 cups **chocolate cookie
dough ice cream**, softened
2 tablespoons **runny caramel
sauce** or **dulce de leche**
(optional)

**To decorate**
**white chocolate** shavings
**milk chocolate** shavings

**Mix** the crushed cookies with the melted butter, then press firmly into the bottom of 4 dessert dishes.

**Scoop** the ice cream over the top of the cookie bases. Drizzle with the caramel or spoon over the dulce de leche, if using, and decorate with white and milk chocolate shavings. Serve immediately.

**For chocolate sundaes with raspberries**, replace the crushed cookies with 20 mini meringues and omit the butter. Layer the ice cream, meringues, and 1 ½ cups raspberries in serving glasses. Drizzle with light cream and top with grated chocolate.

# fruit fritters

Serves **2**
Preparation time **15 minutes**
Cooking time **10 minutes**

6 tablespoons **all-
  purpose flour**
pinch of **ground mixed spice**
pinch of **salt**
1 **egg**, separated
1 tablespoon **butter**, melted
5 tablespoons
  **sparkling water**
**vegetable oil**, for deep-frying
1 firm, ripe **banana**
1 firm, ripe **peach** or **nectarine**
1 crisp **dessert apple**
**confectioners' sugar**, to dust

**Mix** the flour with a pinch of mixed spice and salt in a bowl. Beat in the egg yolk, melted butter, and sparkling water to make a smooth batter.

**Whisk** the egg white in a clean, dry bowl until stiff peaks form, then gently fold into the batter.

**Heat** 1 inch of vegetable oil in a deep heavy saucepan or deep-fat fryer until hot, 350°C, or until a cube of bread dropped into the oil browns in 30 seconds.

**Peel** and thickly slice the banana, meanwhile, then pit and slice the peach, and core and thickly slice the apple.

**Dip** the slices of fruit into the batter and deep-fry for 1–2 minutes, in batches, until crisp and golden. Drain on kitchen towels.

**Dust** the fritters with a little confectioners' sugar and serve piping hot with ice cream.

**For apple fritters with berry sauce**, thaw 1 cup frozen mixed blackberries, raspberries, and cherries, then purée in a blender or food processor with 2 tablespoons confectioners' sugar, or rub through a strainer. Pour into a pitcher. Make up the fritter batter as above and use to coat 3 cored and sliced apples. Deep-fry as above. Dust with confectioners' sugar and serve piping hot with the berry sauce.

# orchard fruit crumble

Serves **6**
Preparation time **20 minutes**
Cooking time **30–35 minutes**

2 **dessert apples**
2 ripe **pears**
13 oz **red plums**, quartered
  and pitted
2 tablespoons **water**
1/3 cup **superfine sugar**
1 cup **all-purpose flour**
1/4 cup **unsalted butter**, diced
2/3 cup **shredded coconut**
1/3 cup **milk chocolate chips**

**Peel**, core, and quarter the apples and pears. Slice the quarters and add the slices to a 5 cup pie dish. Add the plums and the measurement water, then sprinkle with 2 tablespoons of the sugar. Cover the dish with foil and bake in a preheated oven, 350°F, for 10 minutes.

**Put** the remaining sugar in a bowl with the flour, add the butter, and blend with your fingertips or an electric mixer until the mixture resembles fine bread crumbs. Stir in the coconut and chocolate chips.

**Remove** the foil from the fruit and spoon the crumble over the top. Bake for 20–25 minutes until the crumble topping is golden brown and the fruit is tender. Serve warm with custard or cream.

**For plum & orange crumble**, put 1 1/2 lb plums, quartered and pitted, into a 5 cup pie dish with 1/4 cup superfine sugar, omitting the apples and pears. Make the crumble as above, adding the grated zest of 1 small orange and 1/2 cup ground almonds instead of the shredded coconut and chocolate chips. Bake as above.

# caffè latte custards

Serves **6**

Preparation time **20 minutes**, plus chilling

Cooking time **30 minutes**

2 **eggs**

2 **egg yolks**

13 oz can **sweetened condensed milk**

¾ cups **strong black coffee**

⅔ cup **heavy cream**

**unsweetened cocoa powder** to dust

**chocolate wafer cookies,** to serve

**Whisk** together the eggs, egg yolks, and condensed milk in a bowl until just combined. Gradually whisk in the coffee until blended.

**Strain** the mixture through a strainer, then pour into 6 small greased coffee cups. Transfer the cups to a roasting pan. Pour enough hot water into the pan to come halfway up the sides of the cups, then cook in a preheated oven, 325°F, for 30 minutes until just set.

**Lift** the cups out of the water, allow to cool on a wire rack, then transfer to the refrigerator and chill for 4–5 hours.

**Whip** the cream until it forms soft swirls, when ready to serve. Spoon the cream over the top of the desserts, dust with a little sifted cocoa powder, and serve with the chocolate wafer cookies.

**For dark chocolate custards**, bring 1¾ cups milk and ⅔ cup heavy cream just to a boil in a saucepan. Remove from the heat and add 7 oz plain dark chocolate, broken into pieces; allow to melt. In a bowl, whisk together 2 eggs plus 2 egg yolks with ¼ cup superfine sugar and ¼ teaspoon ground cinnamon until light and creamy. Gradually mix in the chocolate mixture and stir until smooth. Strain into small dishes and bake as above. Top with softly whipped cream and chocolate curls.

# drinks

# sea breeze

Makes **2**
Preparation time **3 minutes**

**ice cubes**
2 measures **vodka**
4 measures **cranberry juice**
2 measures **grapefruit juice**
**lime wedges**, to decorate

**Fill** 2 highball glasses with ice cubes, pour over the vodka, cranberry juice, and grapefruit juice and stir well.

**Decorate** with lime wedges and serve with straws for drinking, if desired.

**For bay breeze**, a sweeter drink, replace the grapefruit juice with 2 measures pineapple juice, which contrasts well with the slightly bitter taste of the cranberry juice.

# mojito

Makes **2**
Preparation time **3 minutes**

16 **mint leaves** (including
stalks), plus extra sprigs
to decorate
1 **lime**, cut into wedges
4 teaspoons **cane sugar**
crushed **ice**
5 measures **white rum**
**soda water**, to top up

**Muddle** the mint leaves, lime, and sugar in the bottom
of 2 highball glasses using a muddling stick or a long-
handled teaspoon, gently pressing down and stirring to
release the flavors. Fill the glasses with crushed ice.

**Add** the rum, stir, and top up with soda water.

**Decorate** with mint sprigs and serve.

**For limon mojito**, a citrus version of the classic
mojito, muddle 2 lime quarters with 4 teaspoons
brown sugar and 16 mint leaves in the bottom of
2 highball glasses. Add crushed ice and replace the
white rum with 4 measures Limon Bacardi. Stir and
top up with soda water, if desired. Decorate with lemon
and lime slices and drink through straws.

# hawaiian vodka

Serves **1**
Preparation time **3 minutes**

4–5 **ice cubes**
1 teaspoon **grenadine**
1 measure **pineapple juice**
juice of **1 lemon**
juice of **1 orange**
3 measures **vodka**
slice of **lemon**, to decorate

**Put** the ice cubes in a highball glass and drizzle over the grenadine. Mix together the pineapple, lemon, and orange juices and add to the glass with the vodka.

**Alternatively**, put the ice cubes in a cocktail shaker or screw-top jar. Pour the grenadine, fruit juices and vodka over the ice and shake until a frost forms. Strain into a highball glass.

**Decorate** with a lemon slice and serve.

**For a non-alcoholic Hawaiian cocktail**, mix together 2 measures pineapple juice, 2 measures mango juice, the juice of 1 lemon, and the juice of 1 orange in a pitcher. Pour 1 teaspoon grenadine over ice cubes in a tall glass, then pour over the fruit juice.

# sangria

Serves **10**

Preparation time **8 minutes**, plus chilling

20–30 **ice cubes**

2 x 75 cl bottles **light Spanish red wine**, chilled

½ cup **brandy** (optional)

1¾ cup **soda water**, chilled

slices of **fruit** such as **apples, pears, oranges, lemons, peaches,** and **strawberries**

slices of **orange**, to decorate

**Put** the ice in a large serving pitcher, and pour over the wine and brandy, if using. Give everything a stir.

**Add** the soda water and the slices of fruit. Leave, covered, in the refrigerator until you wish to serve.

**Decorate** the side of each glass with an orange slice, pour in the sangria, and serve.

**For white sangria**, mix 2 x 75 cl bottles Spanish white wine such as Rioja with the brandy and 6 tablespoons superfine sugar. Stir until the sugar has dissolved, then add the ice, soda water, fruit, and sprigs of mint.

# hangover express

Serves **1**
Preparation time **5 minutes**

1 cup **broccoli florets**
2 **dessert apples**, cored and
   quartered
3 cups **spinach**
**ice cubes**

**Juice** the broccoli, apples, and spinach in a juicer or blender, alternating the spinach with the broccoli and apple so that the machine does not get clogged up with the leaves.

**Mix** with a couple of ice cubes before serving, to dilute slightly, as this juice is very sweet.

**For broccoli & express**, juice the broccoli and dessert apples, then stir in 1 tablespoon fresh lemon juice. Serve with ice.

# hot chocolate

Serves **4**
Preparation time **10 minutes**
Cooking time **15 minutes**

4 oz good-quality **bittersweet chocolate**, broken into small pieces
2 tablespoons **superfine sugar**
3 cups **milk**
a few drops of **vanilla extract**
pinch of **ground cinnamon**
3 tablespoons **Kahlua** or other **coffee liqueur** (optional)
**mini marshmallows**, to serve

**Put** the chocolate and sugar in a heavy saucepan. Pour in the milk, then add the vanilla extract and cinnamon.

**Cover** and gently heat, whisking once or twice, until the chocolate has melted. Continue heating until the mixture is steaming hot, but do not allow to boil. Stir in the Kahlua or other coffee liqueur, if desired.

**Ladle** the hot chocolate into 4 large cups or mugs and top with a few mini marshmallows. Serve immediately while steaming hot.

**For peppermint hot chocolate**, melt the chocolate in the milk as above, omitting the vanilla and cinnamon. Replace the coffee liqueur with 3 tablespoons peppermint liqueur, or for a non-alcoholic version use a couple of drops of good-quality natural peppermint extract instead. Divide the hot chocolate among 4 mugs, and top with swirls of freshly whipped cream or extra thick heavy cream, omitting the marshmallows. Hang a peppermint candy cane from the edge of each of the mugs for stirring and crunching and serve immediately.

# banana & peanut butter smoothie

Serves **1**

Preparation time **10 minutes**, plus freezing

1 ripe **banana**
1¼ cups **lowfat milk**
1 tablespoon **smooth peanut butter** or 2 teaspoons **tahini**

**Peel** and slice the banana, put it in a freezerproof container, and freeze for at least 2 hours or overnight.

**Put** the banana, milk, and peanut butter or tahini in a food processor or blender and process until smooth.

**Pour** the smoothie into a tall glass and serve immediately.

**For banana almond smoothie**, put 2 frozen bananas, 1¾ cups soy milk, 1/3 cup ground almonds and a pinch of ground cinnamon in a food processor or blender. Process briefly until smooth.

# the rehydrator

Serves **1**
Preparation time **10 minutes**

**1 orange**
¼ cup **cucumber**
½ cup **cranberry juice**
**ice cubes**

**Peel** the orange, leaving on as much pith as possible. Using a juicer or blender, juice the orange and cucumber until smooth.

**Mix** the orange and cucumber juice with the cranberry juice, then pour into a tall glass over ice. Serve with cucumber stick stirrers.

**For strawberry rehydrator**, omit the cucumber and juice the orange with 1 fresh strawberries. Mix with the cranberry juice and 1½ cups teaspoon clear honey, blending or stirring until the honey has dissolved.

# mind bath

Serves **1**
Preparation time **5 minutes**

1 ½ cups **lettuce**, leaves torn
  or roughly chopped
½ **lemon**, peeled
½ cup **chilled camomile tea**
**ice cubes**

**Juice** the lettuce and lemon using a juicer or blender until smooth.

**Mix** with the chilled camomile tea until well combined. Serve in a glass over ice.

**For pear & ginger mind bath**, omit the lettuce and juice 2 cored and quartered dessert pears and a 1.5 cm ½ inch piece of peeled fresh ginger root until smooth. Mix with the chilled camomile tea.

# index

# acknowledgments

**Executive Editor:** Eleanor Maxfield
**Editor:** Joanne Wilson
**Copy Editor:** Siobhan O'Connor
**Americanizer:** Nicole Foster
**Picture Manager:** Jennifer Veall
**Editorial Assistant:** Diana Copeland
**Senior Designer:** Juliette Norsworthy
**Design and Art Direction:** Tracy Killick
**Photographer:** Stephen Conroy
**Home economist:** Sara Lewis

**Props stylist:** Kim Sullivan
**Senior Production Controller:** Caroline Alberti
**Special photography:** © Octopus Publishing Group Limited/Stephen Conroy
**Other photography:** © Octopus Publishing/David Munns 13, 39, 51, 53, 69, 97, 113, 141, 163, 171; Ian Wallace 16-17, 101, 152-3, 182-3, 199; Lis Parsons 45, 103, 109, 131, 155, 169, 231; Sean Myers 165, 181; Will Heap 5, 191, 197, 201, 213, 215; William Reavell 145; William Shaw 41, 193